FEEL FREE

FEEL FREE

CONQUERING THE EMOTIONS THAT HOLD YOU CAPTIVE

JOSHUA COPRON

ISBN-13: 9780578355825 (Copron)

To protect the privacy of those who have shared their stories with the author, some details and names have been changed.

DEDICATION

Remember all those times you opened up a book and wished someone had dedicated a book to you? Let this be your moment... I dedicate this book to *you,* because you're awesome. Now you no longer need to feel envious. You're welcome.

SPECIAL THANKS

To Sharon, to Jaime, to Brynn, to all those who make me look and sound better than I am. Thank you for using your gifts on my behalf.

FEEL FREE

CONTENTS

FEEL FREE

INTRODUCTION

I once heard a story about a really old zoo in Germany. The animals in this zoo did not have enclosures reflecting their native habitats like the zoos we visit today. Instead, each animal lived between concrete floors and metal bars. This zoo had a giant black bear that had been in one of these small cages for years. All day long this bear would walk thirteen steps to the left and then turn and walk thirteen steps to the right.

Just thirteen steps.

Back and forth.

Eventually, he wore a groove into the concrete floor.

Many people grew concerned for the bear's welfare. People complained and boycotted the zoo, citing the small cage as cruel and inhumane treatment. Worried about backlash from the community, the zoo purchased a neighboring property. This land would provide a habitat like the bear would have in the wild. He could swim through the stream and enjoy a more native environment.

The zoo constructed a fence around the property so visitors could observe the bear. Upon completion, the zoo hosted a huge media promotion to showcase the bear's new habitat. They wanted to spotlight the bear's arrival to this new home where he would be free to roam.

When the day arrived, reporters and animal lovers of all ages crowded together in attendance. Eager to observe the bear in his newly found freedom, they watched as zoo keepers released the bear from the back of the transport.

The giant black bear stepped out of the cage. He turned and walked thirteen steps to the left. Then he walked thirteen steps back to the right. Although the bear was free on the outside, he wasn't free on the inside. The bear's cage was gone, but he didn't *feel free.*

I believe this bear exemplifies the current state of many Christians today. They are free in Christ, yet they don't truly feel free.

In Luke chapter 4, we find Jesus entering the synagogue on the Sabbath Day as was his custom. Synagogue leaders handed him the scroll of Isaiah and He unrolled it to verse 61.

INTRODUCTION

"THE SPIRIT OF THE LORD IS ON ME, BECAUSE HE HAS ANOINTED ME TO PROCLAIM GOOD NEWS TO THE POOR. HE HAS SENT ME TO PROCLAIM FREEDOM FOR THE PRISONERS AND RECOVERY OF SIGHT FOR THE BLIND, TO SET THE OPPRESSED FREE, TO PROCLAIM THE YEAR OF THE LORD'S FAVOR." THEN HE ROLLED UP THE SCROLL, GAVE IT BACK TO THE ATTENDANT AND SAT DOWN. THE EYES OF EVERYONE IN THE SYNAGOGUE WERE FASTENED ON HIM. HE BEGAN BY SAYING TO THEM, "TODAY THIS SCRIPTURE IS FULFILLED IN YOUR HEARING."

LUKE 4:18-21 NIV

This was the passage Jesus read to announce the beginning of His public ministry. This passage in Isaiah 61 is the mission statement of Jesus' ministry on the earth. If you were to sum up this passage in one word, it would be freedom. Jesus came to set people free. Everything Jesus did through His ministry, the cross and resurrection was to unlock prison doors and set us free. Still, many of us, like the bear, don't feel free. We continue to walk the same steps: thirteen steps left and thirteen steps right.

Jesus doesn't just want you to be free; He wants you to feel free. In fact, if you aren't free in your emotions, then you aren't really free at all. If you're bound by guilt, shame, and condemnation, you aren't free. If fear, worry, and anxiety fill your mind, you're not living in freedom. If you are shackled to bitterness, jealousy, and envy, then you haven't stepped outside the door Jesus has already opened. The freedom Jesus came to give each of us can be felt. It is a freedom you can experience in your emotions.

FOR THE KINGDOM OF GOD IS NOT A MATTER OF EATING AND DRINKING, BUT OF ***RIGHTEOUSNESS***, ***PEACE*** AND ***JOY*** IN THE HOLY SPIRIT.

ROMANS 14:7 NIV *EMPHASIS ADDED*

In this verse, two-thirds of God's kingdom is described as emotional. Following Jesus is supposed to have a profound impact on your emotions. Nehemiah 8:10 says the joy of the Lord is your strength. You can't walk in God's strength and victory without having the right emotions.

BUT THE FRUIT OF THE SPIRIT IS LOVE, JOY, PEACE, PATIENCE, KINDNESS, GOODNESS, FAITHFULNESS, GENTLENESS, SELF-CONTROL; AGAINST SUCH THINGS THERE IS NO LAW.
GALATIANS 5:22-23 NASB

The fruit of the Spirit is emotional. A spirit-led life will impact your feelings. God doesn't want you to just be free. He wants you to feel free. Why? Because He knows this: as your emotions go, so goes your life.

In these pages, you will discover the tools needed to not only be free but to live and Feel Free!

PART 1

BREAK FREE

FEEL FREE 1

THE ROLE OF EMOTIONS

I love food. The problem is I don't love healthy food. I love junk food, and I know if I'm going to be healthy, it all starts with what I eat. The problem for me is healthy food is so bland and boring. On one of my many attempts to be healthier, I purchased some groceries that were out of the norm for me. I bought quinoa, which is only good when it is served with something else that is already good. While enjoying a variety of cooking shows, I've never heard anyone say, "This is bland. You know what would kick it up a notch? Quinoa!"

I also bought organic peanut butter because organic food is supposed to be healthy. This is the process I picture when they make organic peanut butter:

1. Start with regular peanut butter.

2. Extract all the all the flavor out of it.

3. Add some oil and peanut grit for texture.

4. Put it back in the jar and label it organic.

Basically, if you want organic peanut butter, just take twenty dollars and throw it in the trash! At least it will save you a trip to the store.

While at the store on this attempt to be healthy, I also bought the now infamous super food: kale. Can we be honest? Kale is disgusting. Now, I can hear those of you who are outraged by that statement. But really, kale tastes like eating a bush out of the backyard. It is only edible when covered in bacon. Don't even get me started on milk. Someone told me we're not supposed to drink milk. He said, "Did you know humans are the only mammals who drink another species' milk? No other species does that." I said, "That's probably because no other species can milk a cow!"

Even though I despise eating healthy, I know if I want to be physically healthy, I need to eat better. This is a fact we all know; however, your diet is not the only thing impacting your physical health. Your emotions also affect your physical health and the overall quality of your life. 3 John 2 says "Beloved, I pray that you may prosper in all things and be in health, just as your soul prospers."

When the Bible speaks of your soul, it's referring to your mind, will, and emotions. Your ability to prosper in every area of your life is connected to the prosperity of your soul. It's connected to the quality of your emotional life. You can't live a prosperous life with negative emotions because as your emotions go, so goes your life.

SPIRIT, SOUL, AND BODY

You are not just a physical and spiritual being; you are an emotional being as well. Each area of your life has needs. When those needs are not being met, each area sends signals informing you of the deficit. The signals tell you attention is needed.

For example, physically you need food to survive. If the physical need for food is not being met, your body sends signals (hunger) to get you to pay attention to this need. If you continue to ignore what your body requires, at some point, it will cause damage to your physical health.

Spiritually, you desire intimacy with God. Your spirit longs for communion with God. Even a life full of achievements will never meet the spiritual void inside of us all. God is the only one who can fulfill your spiritual needs. When the craving for intimacy with God is not being met, your spirit will alert you to pay attention to these needs.

AS YOUR EMOTIONS GO, SO GOES YOUR LIFE.

THE ROLE OF EMOTIONS

Your soul also has needs. When these go unmet, your soul sends signals in the form of emotions to get you to pay attention to these areas. Bitterness, anger, fear, and worry are emotional signs. Your emotions aren't the problem. Emotions are signals alerting you to the fact something is wrong and needs your attention.

Emotions aren't a bad thing. It's not a sin to be emotional. God has emotions, and you are created in God's image and likeness which means you were designed to have emotions. Emotions are a good thing! Understand, the goal is not to eliminate your emotions. God gave them to you for a reason. Your emotions are designed to be indicators.

CHECK ENGINE LIGHT

A friend of mine drove an older car and the check engine light kept popping up on the dashboard. He got so tired of looking at it that he covered it up with a piece of black tape and kept on driving. Sure enough, his car broke down. When he finally took it to a repair shop, the mechanic informed him that if he had come months earlier, the problem would have been easy to fix. It would have cost him less than thirty dollars. Now, since he neglected to have it serviced, the problem had snowballed. The other issues caused by the neglected issue would cost thousands in repairs, and the car wasn't even worth that much! He ended up totaling his car all because he didn't want to be bothered by the check engine light.

Your feelings are like the check engine light on a dashboard. They are signals prompting you to give your attention to a problem. Dashboard lights aren't the issue. They are signals. They are alerting you to a problem you otherwise wouldn't have noticed. Emotions serve you as God's warning lights alerting you that something in your life needs attention.

If you're feeling bitter, ignoring it will not solve the problem. You need to investigate. Why? Bitterness is a check engine light illuminating the need to forgive. If you keep driving and overlook it, you will eventually get stuck because you ignored the warning light. If you're feeling angry, don't neglect that indicator. Anger is a secondary emotion. You need to look under the hood and see what's going on before you blow a gasket. If you're feeling discouraged, you can't afford to ignore the feeling. You need to examine why. Neglecting the thirty dollar discouragement can lead to thousands of dollars spent dealing with depression.

INDICATORS NOT DICTATORS

Emotions are indicators. They are warning lights to help you understand attention is needed in a particular area. The problem is when emotions move from being indicators to dictators. Having emotions is a good thing. Being led by your emotions isn't a good thing. God created you to live with feelings, but you shouldn't be led by them. Your feelings should serve you, but you shouldn't serve your feelings. Feelings make great servants but horrible masters. Emotions are like kids. You can't put them in the driver's seat, but you can't put them in the trunk either. No matter how annoying they become, you can't do it. I know some of you parents have thought about it, but it's illegal. Emotions, like kids, need to be in the car just in the right place. Emotions should not be in control of your life, but you can't ignore them either. You shouldn't put your feelings in charge of your decisions, but you also can't neglect them. They need to be put in their proper place.

THE PROBLEM IS WHEN EMOTIONS MOVE FROM BEING INDICATORS TO DICTATORS.

It's okay to have emotions. Just don't let emotions have you. It's okay to be jealous. Just don't let jealousy have you. It's okay to be afraid. Just don't let fear have you. It's okay to grieve. Just don't let grief have you.

Having feelings is one thing. But when your feelings have you, you can get in trouble. When you fail to manage your emotions, you end up mismanaging your life.

Imagine buying a brand new car and as you are driving off the lot and a man rear-ends you. You get so angry that you punch the man in the face. Then the police then show up and see you hitting this man. They arrest you for assault and throw you in jail. Just to make it worse, imagine before you left work that day, your boss said, "If you miss one more day, you are fired." And your spouse said, "If you lose this job, I'm going to leave you." And because you are in jail for twenty-four hours, you end up missing work the next day and you get fired. When your spouse hears about it, she leaves you. Now you are sitting in jail thinking, "How did I get here?"

Your emotions took you there. You want to sit there and blame the devil, but the devil didn't do it. You did it. Instead of managing your emotions, you allowed your emotions to dictate your decisions. Your failure to manage your emotions drove you right to your current situation. You may find yourself in a situation thinking "How did I get here?" Nine out of ten times your emotions took you there.

How did you end up with so much debt? Your emotions led the way. I heard a story about this man who sat down and talked to his wife about her shopping habits. He sat her down and said, "You can't buy any more new clothes." She understood that it was a problem and she agreed not to buy any more new clothes. The next day she was at the mall and she had her mind made up that she wasn't going to buy anything. She was just going to look. Then she saw this beautiful dress in the window and she said to herself, "I'm not going to buy it. I'm just going to try it on to see how it looks." One thing led to another, and she ended up buying the dress.

She got home and her husband said, "I thought we had a deal. You weren't going to buy any more clothes. She said, "Honey, I'm so sorry. When I tried the dress on, the enemy tempted me and I just couldn't resist." He said, "Why didn't you do what the Bible says and say, "Get behind me Satan?" She said, "I did. I said, "Get behind me Satan." And he told me, "The dress looks even better from behind."

THE ROLE OF EMOTIONS

You can behave completely contrary to what you set out to do when you allow yourself to be governed by your feelings. The vast majority of times we end up in places you never wanted to be, it's because you allowed your emotions to take the lead. When your feelings manage you, you end up mismanaging your life.

FEEL FREE

2

IN MY FEELS

We are designed to live with emotions, but we aren't meant to be led by our emotions. Sadly, many allow emotions to dictate the daily decisions of their lives. Our culture even has a phrase for this: "I'm just in my feels." When you are in your feels, you defer to your feelings as your guide for decisions and choices. It's when your emotions are the vehicle moving you through life.

In many ways our culture encourages us to live this way. "Be true to yourself." "Follow your heart." "Live your truth." Yet, living your truth is usually not truth. It's whatever feels right to you in the moment. Culture encourages us to follow our feelings. But have you ever met anyone who was prospering in life who did whatever they felt like doing? I haven't.

Imagine if you woke up one day and didn't feel like going to work, so you called your boss and said, "I'm not coming in to work this week. I'm not sick. I just don't feel like working." If you did that, you wouldn't have a job. Imagine if you called your spouse and said, "I'm not coming home tonight. I just don't feel like it. I'm going to someone else's house." You might not have a spouse anymore if you did that.

Parents, think of your children —the ones living under your roof, eating your food and spending your money. If you tell them to wash the dishes and they say, "No, I don't feel like it," your response might be something to the effect of, "I don't care how you feel. You'd better wash those dishes because you are replaceable. I can make another kid that looks justlike you and have a lot of fun doing it."

Allowing your emotions to call the shots and be in charge of your actions is a sure-fire way to ruin your life. Don't allow your emotions to be your Uber in life. They'll end up driving you on a longer route that costs more while taking you somewhere you never intended to go.

SO I'M TELLING YOU THIS, AND I INSIST ON IT IN THE LORD: YOU SHOULDN'T LIVE YOUR LIFE LIKE THE GENTILES ANYMORE. THEY BASE THEIR LIVES ON POINTLESS THINKING, AND THEY ARE IN THE DARK IN THEIR REASONING. THEY ARE DISCONNECTED FROM GOD'S LIFE BECAUSE

OF THEIR IGNORANCE AND THEIR CLOSED HEARTS. THEY ARE PEOPLE WHO LACK ALL SENSE OF RIGHT AND WRONG, AND WHO HAVE TURNED THEMSELVES OVER TO DOING WHATEVER FEELS GOOD AND TO PRACTICING EVERY SORT OF CORRUPTION ALONG WITH GREED. BUT YOU DIDN'T LEARN THAT SORT OF THING FROM CHRIST.
EPHESIANS 4:17-20 CEB

When your life becomes dominated by your feelings, you do whatever feels right in the moment. You yield to every feeling and desire. Living this way is guaranteed to sabotage your success, undermine your joy, destroy your potential, and derail God's destiny for your life.

MOSES

Moses led the Israelites out of slavery in Egypt. Moses is listed in Hebrews 11 as an example of faith. In all of Israel's history, there were no other prophets or leaders with the same face-to-face relationship that Moses had with God (Deuteronomy 34:10-12). Yet, because of his inability to control his anger, Moses never got to enter the Promised Land.

In Numbers 20, the Israelites were near the end of their forty years of wandering in the desert. When the people were out of water, Moses asked God, "What do we do?" The instructions Moses received were to gather the people and speak to a rock then water would come forth.

This was significant because before this, God had spoken to Moses and told him to strike the rock (Exodus 17). This time God was telling him to simply *speak* to the rock. Instead of listening to God, Moses got angry with the people. Moses struck the rock with his staff instead of speaking to it. Because of this inability to control his anger, Moses wasn't allowed to enter the Promised Land.

You might be thinking, "That sounds like a harsh punishment." Understand this, Moses messed up an important analogy God was trying to illustrate. The water-giving rock was a symbol of Christ (1 Corinthians 10:4). The rock was struck once in Exodus 17:6, just like Christ was struck with your sin on the cross. Moses speaking to the rock was to illustrate how Jesus only needed to die once. Now, all you have to do is speak and ask Jesus Christ to come into your life.

Jesus was struck once and He continues to offer living water to all who call upon Him. In his anger, Moses struck the rock and destroyed the Biblical typology. Moses couldn't enter the Promised Land because he allowed his anger to control him. Your emotions, if not in check, can derail your destiny. Even worse, your emotions can destroy your life.

JUDAS

Judas was one of Jesus' twelve disciples. As one of the twelve, he got to spend more time with Jesus than anyone outside of that group. Nonetheless, Judas betrayed Jesus for thirty pieces of silver.

WHEN JUDAS, WHO HAD BETRAYED HIM, SAW THAT JESUS WAS CONDEMNED, HE WAS SEIZED WITH REMORSE AND RETURNED THE THIRTY PIECES OF SILVER TO THE CHIEF PRIESTS AND THE ELDERS. "I HAVE SINNED," HE SAID, "FOR I HAVE BETRAYED INNOCENT BLOOD." "WHAT IS THAT TO US?" THEY REPLIED. "THAT'S YOUR RESPONSIBILITY." SO JUDAS THREW THE MONEY INTO THE TEMPLE AND LEFT. THEN HE WENT AWAY AND HANGED HIMSELF.
MATTHEW 27:3-5 NIV

Judas was "seized with remorse". He ignored the check engine light. When Judas got out of his feelings and saw what he had done, he tried to give the money back because it wasn't what he really wanted. When you are led by your emotions, you end up doing things you never wanted to do. Sometimes, you end up doing things you wouldn't have believed yourself capable of doing.

Judas loved Jesus, but he still betrayed him. You may be thinking, "How do you know Judas loved Jesus?" Look at the remorse Judas felt after he betrayed him. He tried to return the thirty pieces of silver, but he was so anguished by his decision that he hung himself. You don't end your life over decisions that hurt people you don't care about. Judas didn't say, "He'll get over it. It's no big deal." No, that wasn't Judas' attitude because he loved Jesus.

You can love someone greatly, but when you act out of your feelings, you can end up betraying them. Judas' emotions drove him to make a decision that not only hurt Jesus but also hurt himself. Although it was a horrible act, Judas ended up killing himself over something that could have been forgiven.

THE WORD AND THE SPIRIT

This is what happens when you allow your emotions to take the lead. Your feelings move from being clues to commanders. Your feelings manage you and you end up mismanaging your life. Feelings derail you from God's destiny for your life and drive you to make decisions that destroy your future.

You cannot step into God's best for your life if you are stuck in your feelings. God never intended for your life to be guided and governed by your emotions. God's plan is for your life to be guided and governed by His Word and His Spirit.

SO GET RID OF ALL THE FILTH AND EVIL IN YOUR LIVES, AND HUMBLY ACCEPT THE WORD GOD HAS PLANTED IN YOUR HEARTS, FOR IT HAS THE POWER TO SAVE YOUR SOULS.
JAMES 1:21 NLT

The moment you come to faith in Jesus, your spirit is made new. When you go to heaven, you will receive a new glorified body free from the effects of sin. So your spirit is saved, your body *will be* saved, and your soul is *being* saved. The process of salvation is being worked out in your soul on a daily basis. Your mind, will, and emotions need to be continually transformed.

YOUR EMOTIONS, IF NOT IN CHECK, CAN DERAIL YOUR DESTINY.

Since you still feel things that aren't godly, think thoughts that aren't pure and desire things that aren't good. Because of this you will need to bring your mind, will, and emotions under the influence of His Word and His Spirit. This is a life-long process.

FEEL FREE 3

AWARENESS

There was once a baby camel who was curiously checking out his body. The baby camel said, "Mom, why do we have these big paws with three toes?" She said, "That's so we don't sink into the sand." He said, "Mom, why do we have these big eye lashes?" She said, "Sometimes, it gets windy in the desert and the wind blows the sand into our eyes. These big eye lashes keep the sand out." He said, "Why do we have these big humps on our backs?" She said, "The humps store fat so that we can travel long distances through the desert when food is scarce."

The baby camel said, "So, we have paws so we don't sink through the sand in the desert, we have eye lashes to keep the desert sand out of our eyes, and we have humps to travel long distances through the desert?" The mother said, "That's right." He said, "Then why we do live in the zoo?"

Can you relate to the baby camel? You know you were born to be free, but you end up caged by destructive feelings and imprisoned by negative emotions. How can you break free? The first step to finding freedom starts with awareness. You can't adjust what you won't acknowledge. You can't fix what you won't face. You can't conquer what you won't confront. However, if you'll face destructive feelings for a season, you can leave them for a lifetime. The other option is quite the opposite: You can remain in bondage for a lifetime to avoid facing those feelings for a season. You can't find freedom from negative emotions if you aren't aware of the emotions holding you in bondage.

> YOU CAN'T FIND FREEDOM FROM NEGATIVE EMOTIONS IF YOU AREN'T AWARE OF THE EMOTIONS HOLDING YOU IN BONDAGE.

Remember shopping at the mall? If you were looking for a specific store, you would stop at the directory (the giant sign with all the stores and their locations). The most important thing on that sign is the star that says, "You are here." It's only when you recognize where you are that you can begin to move in the right direction.

The same is true for your emotions. When you recognize what

emotions you are feeling, you can begin to move in the right direction to get free. You can't get free if you don't know you are bound. And yes, it is possible to be in bondage and not even realize it!

> JESUS SAID TO THE JEWS WHO HAD BELIEVED HIM, "IF YOU HOLD TO MY TEACHING, YOU ARE REALLY MY DISCIPLES. THEN YOU WILL KNOW THE TRUTH, AND THE TRUTH WILL SET YOU FREE." THEY ANSWERED HIM, "WE ARE ABRAHAM'S DESCENDANTS AND HAVE NEVER BEEN SLAVES OF ANYONE. HOW CAN YOU SAY THAT WE SHALL BE SET FREE?"
>
> JOHN 8:31-33 NIV

Jesus says, "You will know the truth and the truth will set you free." The Jews replied with one of the funniest statements in the entire Bible. Think about it: They said, "We are Abraham's descendants and have *never* been in bondage of anyone. How can you say that we shall be set free?"

Have you read the Old Testament? The Israelites had been in bondage to *everyone*: the Chaldeans, the Babylonians, the Assyrians, and the Egyptians. They even celebrated celebrated Passover to remember when they were in bondage in Egypt and how God had set them free. In fact, they were in bondage to the Romans when they made the statement "How can you say we shall be set free?"

Like the Israelites, you may have a hard time admitting when you are in bondage. You may have a difficult time realizing you are enslaved to destructive emotions. You may lack the self awareness needed to move forward in a journey to lasting freedom.

At times, you may not even recognize the envy and comparison you live with every day. You may not perceive the shame you carry with you everywhere you go. The worry and anxiety dictating all your decisions may feel like a normal part of life. Bitterness and resentment ends up poisoning your attitude and all your relationsips along with it and feels like it is a part of you. It's almost like you wouldn't know how to live without it because you've grown so accustom to those negative feelings.

BLIND SPOTS

Everyone experiences blind spots in life. You are not the exception to this reality. The concept of blind spots is most familiar when it comes to driving. When looking in the mirrors of a car, there are blind spots, or places where you can't see everything You may have cut someone off while driving because you didn't see them. Some of us have even crashed into another car because it was in a blind spot.

The thing about blind spots is while you may not be able to see them, others around you can. The spots may be blind to you, but they are obvious to everyone else. This is why we all need community and accountability. We need people in our lives who will point out our blind spots or as Ephesians 4:15 calls it "speak the truth in love." The reason we need people to speak the truth to us is because we have an incredible capacity to live in denial.

For example, couples who don't have children think they know what it's like to have children. They talk to each other about it: "I can't wait for us to have a family. You'll be such a good dad. I think you'll be an amazing mom. Wouldn't it be so wonderful to have little versions of us running around the house?"

They actually believe they know what they're talking about. Until you have children of your own, who live in your home twenty-four seven, you have no idea what it's like. You can't possibly know how difficult simple everyday tasks will become. Things you do without much thought or effort will become impossible. For example, leaving the house is no longer easy. When you don't have kids and you want to leave the house, you simply walk out the door. When you do have kids and want to leave the house, you must prepare for the inevitable battle to even make it to the car.

"Kids, get your shoes."

"I don't know where they are."

"Where did you last see them?"

"On my feet!"

When you have kids, leaving the house is full of stress and mental checklists. If you don't have kids, you can't understand this daily struggle. You don't know what you don't know.

We all have blind spots. The key to getting rid of them is having people in our lives who can speak the truth in love and are willing to point out our blind spots. Without those people our capacity for denial is enormous. It's only when confronted with the truth of your emotional blind spots that you can experience freedom.

"YOU WILL KNOW THE TRUTH, AND THE TRUTH WILL SET YOU FREE."
JOHN 8:32 NIV

If truth sets you free, then deception keeps you in bondage. To the degree that you live in deception, or are blind to your negative emotions, you will remain imprisoned by them. You cannot adjust what you continue to ignore. It's only when you are face-to-face with the truth that you can experience freedom. Feeling free begins with an awareness of the places in your life where you aren't free. Becoming aware of the negative emotions holding you back is just the first step to feeling free. Next, you have to take ownership of those feelings.

FEEL FREE 4

OWNERSHIP

Once you become aware of the negative emotions keeping you in bondage, the next step in feeling free is ownership. In order to improve it, you must first own it. Taking ownership can be a little problematic. It is much easier to transfer ownership of how you feel to other people. You say things like, "He put me in a bad mood. She didn't make me happy. He made me so mad. She drives me crazy."

If he put you in a bad mood, if she drives you crazy, then there is nothing you can do. After all, someone else made you feel the way you feel. You had nothing to do with it! Now that you've placed the responsibility on someone else, you've told yourself there's nothing you can do about it. Transferring ownership of our emotions locks us in a prison and puts the key in the hands of the other person. By owning your emotions you take the key back and free yourself from the captivity of your feelings.

When you stop engaging in this endless blame game, you can discover the blessing of freedom. When you attribute your negative emotions to others, it anesthetizes the problem area. It keeps you from addressing the issue that's been causing the pain in the first place. Neglecting to identify the source of the cycle will ensure it continues to play on repeat. I'm not sure if you've realized this, but the people blamed for your negative emotions don't often come back and clean up their mess. The ones who broke you will not fix you. The ones who hurt you won't heal you. If you keep waiting for someone else to fix you so you can be free, you'll wait forever. But if you stop casting blame, you can catch the blessing of freedom.

BLAME IS IN OUR DNA

ABOVE ALL ELSE, GUARD YOUR HEART,
FOR EVERYTHING YOU DO FLOWS FROM IT.
PROVERBS 4:23 NIV

The heart is the seat of your emotions. Scripture tells you to guard your heart, but you can't guard what you don't own. If you find yourself unconvinced, you can go ahead and test it out for yourself. Go to your neighbor'd house, put up a big fence with a gate, and lock the gate. See how that plays out when your neighbor gets home and sees someone has locked him out of his own home. You can only guard what you own. Once you own something, it becomes your responsibility to protect and manage it.

No one wants to be controlled by someone else, so why are we so quick to blame others for our feelings? If I can blame someone else, it makes me feel better about me. Plus, it makes for a better story. Sharing a narrative of what "they did" has proven to be more enticing to listeners. Talking about what other people did to you (how awful they were, what mean things they said, etc.) sounds a lot better than "I lost my temper."

> **WHEN YOU ARE REALLY FREE, NO MATTER HOW BADLY YOU WANT TO SAY YES TO SOMETHING, YOU WILL STILL BE ABLE TO SAY NO.**

Talking about what *they* said about you gains sympathy from others. Saying, "I'm really insecure and that's why I let what was said bother me so much" won't get you any sympathy. When you talk about what they did to you, it feels as if you're winning people to your side. Plus, blaming others is in our DNA.

BLAME IN OUR DNA

In Genesis, God put Adam and Eve in the garden. He told

them they could eat from any tree they wanted except for the tree of the knowledge of good and evil. God was teaching them to live within the boundaries He put in place. Real freedom is not revealed in your ability to say yes to whatever you want; it's revealed in your ability to say no. When you are really free, no matter how badly you want to say yes to something, you will still be able to say no.

God was teaching mankind in order to live fully free, you need to live with boundaries. This isn't God restricting you; it's God protecting you. If you know the story, Adam and Eve disobeyed God and ate from the forbidden tree. God asked, "Why did you do the one thing I commanded you not to?"

THE MAN SAID, "THE WOMAN YOU PUT HERE WITH ME—SHE GAVE ME SOME FRUIT FROM THE TREE, AND I ATE IT." THEN THE LORD GOD SAID TO THE WOMAN, "WHAT IS THIS YOU HAVE DONE?" THE WOMAN SAID, "THE SERPENT DECEIVED ME, AND I ATE."
GENESIS 3:12-13 NIV

Bam! Right away, Adam blamed Eve. Eve blamed the serpent and the serpent didn't have a leg to stand on.

That was cheesey, but I couldn't help it. Just like we can't help blaming others. It's part of our current condition. It is woven into our DNA.

I remember when my brother Gabe was about six years old. This particular time, he went to take a shower and became intrigued by an object he normally ignored: my Mom's razor. I've heard of kids mimicking what they've seen their parents do and trying to shave their legs, or maybe even their face, but Gabe went all in. He took that razor straight to his head and shaved three inches from his hair line. With no way to reverse what he had done, he came out of the shower with a giant bald strip right down the middle of his head. Shocked, I asked him, "What did you do?!" The response he chose was, "What? I didn't do anything. It just happened. I was just washing my hair, and it happened."

Even when there is no one to blame but ourselves, we will continue to make up excuses that avoid taking responsibility. We blame others and point our fingers when it comes to our emotional outbursts and bad attitudes. As long as it's someone else's fault, you can avoid having to change.

This is how a victim mentality gains traction in your life. We've all been victims at one time or another. Being hurt by others is a part of living in close proximity to any other person. These emotional wounds can and will happen, but that doesn't mean you can blame others for your own well-being.

There is a difference between a reason and an excuse. A reason is an explanation of cause or justification for an action, while an excuse is an attempt to lessen the blame attached to an offense. Just because the reason you feel the way you do is real doesn't mean the excuse you're using to hold onto that feeling is right. We inherited the tendency to blame others from Adam and Eve, but the DNA of Jesus, the second Adam (1 Corinthians 15:45-49), is also inside of you. Your cells are encoded with the DNA of an overcomer. They put Jesus in the grave and three days later He came out. The grave wasn't Jesus' fault, but the resurrection was His responsibility. Even if it's not your fault, you are still responsible for how you respond.

In saying you need to take responsibility for you how feel, I'm not suggesting you are liable for the situation, nor am I ignoring the contributions another person made to the problem. Taking ownership of your emotions means it may not be your fault, but it is your responsibility. It wasn't your fault you were hurt, betrayed, abused, or abandoned. But how those wounds play out in your daily life is in your hands. You didn't author the situation, but you choose how it's going to impact your life. Realizing your emotions are your responsibility will empower you to put them in their proper place.

SMUGGLER

When your unstable emotions get dragged into your future, they undermine your happiness. Blaming your emotional well-being on others allows you to smuggle negative emotions into your future.

When you go through airport security, there is list of items you aren't allowed to take on a flight. Over the years the list seems to get longer and longer. Apparently, everything can be used a weapon. "Sir, you can't take that lotion on the plane." Lotion? What kind of bomb could you make out of lotion anyway? Even if I could make a lotion bomb and it went off on the plane, the worst that could happen is everyone would have soft skin. You can't even take a drink through airport security. Why? Are they affraid someone may use it to hijack the plane? "Everybody sit down! I'm in control of this plane now. If you don't do what I say, I'll take the cap off of this Coke and everyone is going to get sticky."

Now, while you can't take a Coke through airport security, you can purchase a Coke once you've made it through. Apparently, someone has done the research and they've discovered that $7 Cokes can't be weaponized. If you don't want to pay $7 for a drink, you'd better find a way to smuggle it through security.

Blaming others for your emotional state smuggles those destructive emotions into your future. It's like stuffing them into the bottom of your bag and hoping security won't notice. You're trying to bring something that doesn't belong where you are going.

When emotions aren't checked or properly vetted, you can expect a repeat performance. You may think if it wasn't your fault to begin with so there's nothing you need to change. This makes it impossible to learn from the past. This inability to learn ensures you will repeat the dysfunctional pattern over and over again. You can't blame your way to freedom. The path to feeling free starts with owning your emotions.

OWN IT

This concept may be hard for some people to grasp. You may

think, "I can't help how I feel." But you do, in fact, have control over your emotions. You choose how you will feel and respond in any given situation. Feelings are like waves. You can't stop them from coming, but you can choose which ones to surf.

"MOREOVER ALL THESE CURSES SHALL COME UPON YOU AND PURSUE AND OVERTAKE YOU...BECAUSE YOU DID NOT SERVE THE LORD YOUR GOD WITH JOY AND GLADNESS OF HEART, FOR THE ABUNDANCE OF EVERYTHING,"
DEUTERONOMY 28:45-47 NIV

Deuteronomy 28 explains how the Old Covenant was based on works. If you obeyed God, blessings would come upon you. If you disobeyed God, curses would come upon you. Thankfully, Jesus has secured a new covenant with His people. The New Covenant is one of grace and it isn't based on your ability to adhere to the Old Covenant rules and laws. The New Covenant stands on what Jesus did for us. Jesus has redeemed you from the curse of the law and qualified you to receive every blessing. You don't have to live in fear of curses coming upon you when you disobey. With that being said, I find it interesting that people living under the Old Covenant would experience these curses if they didn't serve God with joy and gladness.

If you could be judged for not serving with joy and gladness, then you must have the ability to choose joy. You can't be judged for something you have no control over. God wouldn't hold you accountable if you didn't have the ability to choose, which means you *do* have the ability to choose it. You have the ability to choose how you will feel in any given situation.

This means you don't have to wake up and see how you feel before you know if you can enjoy your day. It means you can wake up and choose to live with joy and gladness in your heart. You can decide to have a positive attitude today. You can determine to live at peace with others. You have authority over your emotions.

"DO NOT LET YOUR HEARTS BE TROUBLED. YOU BELIEVE IN GOD; BELIEVE ALSO IN ME."
JOHN 14:1 NIV

Jesus said, "Do not let your hearts be troubled." This means you can be in trouble without being troubled within. You can face hardships without letting anger, grief or pain overwhelm you. You can endure adversity and still have joy and peace.

"PATIENCE IS BETTER THAN POWER, AND CONTROLLING ONE'S EMOTIONS, THAN CAPTURING A CITY."
PROVERBS 16:32 NIV

Many people live as if they have no control over their emotions. If they are stuck in a bad attitude, if they are constantly getting upset, if they are hyper-critical of others, if negativity seems to follow them everywhere they go - they will stay in those feelings the entire day, hoping that tomorrow will make them feel better. These people view bad attitudes like a storm; they believe they just have to wait it out and let it pass on. That is simply not true.

Viktor Frankl, a Holocaust survivor, writes about his experience living in a concentration camp. Everything was taken away from him, including his clothes, pictures and personal belongings. The Nazis even took away his name and gave him a number instead. However, there remained one thing the Nazis couldn't take away. Viktor said, "Everything can be taken from a man but one thing: the last of human freedoms - to choose one's attitude in any given set of circumstances."

You can't always control your situation. You can't control what happens to you. The one thing you can control is how you respond. You have the ability to govern your emotions so they don't rule your life. So choose joy regardless of your circumstances. Choose peace even in the midst of trouble. Choose hope rather than fear and worry.

PART 2

WALK FREE

FEEL FREE 5

ATTENTION

At the University of Oklahoma there was a project designed to teach a chimpanzee how to talk using sign language. Over the years Washoe, the subject of this project, learned 140 different signs. One day the project director decided it was time for Washoe to conceptualize. Instead of merely imitating words, the director felt Washoe was ready to express her own thoughts and feelings.

What you need to understand about this chimpanzee is that she was incredibly pampered. She was well fed, had a comfortable living space and was safe from all harm. Despite it all, when she was able to conceptualize her own thoughts and feelings, her first words were, "Let me out." Over and over again she said, "Let me out." She was spoiled with comforts, yet the only thing Washoe wanted was freedom.[1]

Naturally we all long for freedom. No matter how comfortable you are in your bondage, your heart longs to feel free. The freedom God offers isn't the kind where you grit your teeth and try really hard not to allow your emotions to take the lead. His freedom allows you to actually change how you feel.

In order to change your emotions, there are three spiritual laws you need to understand. Spiritual laws are like the natural laws that govern the world. Following and respecting these laws works for you, not against you.

THE LAW OF ATTENTION

Attention spans are getting shorter. We're all watching this reality play out around us. Some say the average attention span has decreased from 12 seconds in the year 2000 to eight seconds in 2020. Goldfish have an attention span of 9 seconds. At this point, goldfish are doing better than we are! Attention spans may be shortening, but what we give our attention to remains important.

The things you pay attention to will grow, while the things you ignore will diminish. The more you focus on something, the larger it becomes in your mind and emotions. Feelings are the result of what you fixate on. Your mood, attitude, and emotions are the result of your focus. You will always feel what you focus on.

FOR AS HE THINKS IN HIS HEART, SO IS HE.
PROVERBS 23:7

There are two types of thoughts: head thoughts and heart thoughts. Head thoughts are all the commonplace thoughts that go through your mind during the day: What am I going to wear? What am I going to make for dinner? What time is my appointment? What do I need to get from the store? Head thoughts are easily forgotten. Can you even remember what you had for lunch four days ago? This kind of stuff is quickly forgotten. There is little need for your mind to store that kind of information. Heart thoughts are different though. Heart thoughts live on the center stage of our minds.

We tend to focus on the betrayal, abandonment, injustice, abuse, trauma, loss, failure, fatigue, or disappointments. It's our heart thoughts that define us and eventually become our reality. Your heart thoughts impact your emotions and what you allow your mind to focus on shapes how you feel. For this very reason, Scripture constantly encourages us to set our minds on things above.

Thinking depressing thoughts will cause you to become depressed. Thinking worried thoughts will cause you to have anxiety. If you continue to think about past mistakes and failures, you will continue to feel guilt and shame. Every time you replay an experience, you are refueling that emotion. As long as you provide the fuel, your feelings will never change. That's why you have to fix your focus. Circumstances cannot always be changed, but you can control what you concentrate on.

Imagine a set of twins. One is a pessimist while the other an optimist. Their parents are concerned and consult with a psychiatrist. "You have to help us. Our twins are about to have their 10th birthday and the pessimist is so negative. If you put him in a dark room, he'd develop. (Get it?) Our other son is so positive it's annoying!" The psychiatrist replies, "On their birthday, give the pessimist the most extravagant gifts. Spare no expense. Get him everything he wants and for the optimist, get him the worst possible present you can imagine."

Their 10th birthday came and the parents got the pessimist the latest Xbox, a new iPhone and a trip to Disney World. A few minutes later, the boy went to his room crying, "This is the worst day of my life. I don't have any new games for my Xbox. If I drop this new iPhone and break the screen I don't have any money to fix it. I know when I go to Disney, I'm going to have to wait in line forever. I wanted the fast pass!" He complained about every single gift and he remained a pessimist.

For the optimist's birthday gifts, they filled his bedroom with manure. The parents thought they would definitely have two crying kids after that. They walked over to the optimist's room and all they saw were two little legs sticking out of the manure. Shocked, they asked "Son, are you okay?" He replied, "Mom! Dad! This is awesome!" Baffled, the parents said, "What could possibly be awesome about all this manure?" The kid answered, "You can't fool me. When there is this much manure, there has to be a pony!"

In every situation, you can choose to either focus on the negative or the positive. How the events of life unfold is beyond your control, but you can determine where you place your focus.

In studying attitude and emotions, Professor Vicki Medvec revealed our focus is more important than our circumstances. She studied Olympic medalists and discovered bronze medalists were happier than silver medalists. Silver medalists were inclined to focus on how close they came to winning gold, so they weren't satisfied with their finish. The bronze medalists tend to focus on how close they came to not winning a medal at all. They were just happy to place.[2]

How you feel isn't based on circumstances. If that were the case, then the silver medalists would always be happier than the bronze medalists because they did better. Nonetheless, your emotions are based on your focus and your focus determines your feelings.

YOUR EMOTIONS ARE BASED ON YOUR FOCUS, AND YOUR FOCUS DETERMINES YOUR FEELINGS

FINALLY, BROTHERS AND SISTERS, WHATEVER IS TRUE, WHATEVER IS NOBLE, WHATEVER IS RIGHT, WHATEVER IS PURE, WHATEVER IS LOVELY, WHATEVER IS ADMIRABLE—IF ANYTHING IS EXCELLENT OR PRAISEWORTHY—THINK ABOUT SUCH THINGS.

ATTENTION

PHILIPPIANS 4:8 NIV

Philippians 4:8 gives us a list of things we should set our minds and hearts on, things that need to fill our focus in order to feel free. In whatever situation we face we can choose to focus on things that are true, noble, right and pure rather than dwelling on every negative thought. The doorway of our mind is under our command. We can't stop all the negative thoughts from knocking on the door of our mind, but we can however determine whether or not we open the door and let them in.

Now, let's journey into the next step toward freeing your mind by discovering how to fill it with the right things.

FOOTNOTES

1. *Paul Harvey, 1980. Chimpanzee Voices Plea.* https://gentleworld.org/chimpanzee-voices-plea/.

2. *Andrew Schroer. 2016. It's all about perspective. Victoria Advocate. https://www.victoriaadvocate.com/news/features/faith/its-all-about-perspective/article_a47990e6-ac57-512f-b61a-84de3a605317.html*

FEEL FREE 6

EXCHANGE

I played basketball back in high school, and a friend once told me by running cross country during the off season, I would be in even better shape for basketball season. You know what I learned? There is nothing fun about cross country. Here is what you do: RUN! I'm not really sure why cross country even needs a coach. His job everyday was to say, "Go!" That's it. At its origin, someone had to know it wasn't a good sport, so they came up with a fake name for it. "Let's call it cross country." It should just be called death by shin splints.

Naming this boring activity "cross country" is misleading. The creators were probably hoping people would say, "Oh, cross country, sounds like we'll be going places." Nope! You're not going anywhere. You are going to the park about a mile from your school and you're going to run circles around it for four months. And you know how you're going to get to the park? You're going to run. As if going to the park to run around it wasn't bad enough, they're also making everyone run just to get there. You won't run 2,800 miles across the country, taking in all the magnificent scenery. Instead, you'll run 2,800 miles around your local park, staring at the same two trees day in and day out, wondering why you signed yourself up for this.

The only thing you do besides run is stretch. They say stretching is really important and if you don't stretch, you can get hurt. How hurt? Hurt enough to where I don't have to run? Sounds good.

As you may have guessed, cross country wasn't for me. I tried it and hated every minute of it. The only thing I could think about when I was running was how much I don't like running. The more I thought about it the more I hated it. When playing basketball though, I could run all day. That's the law of exchange. When playing basketball, I wasn't actually focused on running. I was focused on scoring. When you focus on something positive, it automatically displaces the negative.

THE LAW OF EXCHANGE

The law of exchange means you can't simply do away with a negative thought or emotion. Rather, you have to replace it with something positive. It's not enough to try and stop focusing on negative things; you have to intentionally exchange negative thoughts for positive ones.

Your conscious mind can hold only one thought at a time. That one thought is either going to be life-giving or defeating. Resisting a thought or feeling only drives it deeper into your awareness, causing you to focus on it more. Have you ever been upset with a family member and tried telling yourself not to be upset about what they did? If so, you probably noticed that you were more concentrated on what was irritating you, and your mood ended up worse.

Another example would be if we were playing golf and I said to you, "Don't think about hitting your ball into the sand trap." Of course, you immediately think of doing so. Then you may think, "Okay, I will not hit my ball into the sand trap." But you're still thinking about hitting it in the sand trap! Our minds find it very difficult to concentrate on the reverse of something. If you don't want to hit your ball in the sand trap, don't focus on averting the sand trap. Focus on the fairway, whee you actually want the ball to go.

Negative thoughts are the sand traps, so instead of trying to not think negatively, focus on the positives. Focus on where you want to go. This is what Paul did in Philippians Chapter 3 when he said the following:

EXCHANGE

BROTHERS AND SISTERS, I DO NOT CONSIDER MYSELF YET TO HAVE TAKEN HOLD OF IT. BUT ONE THING I DO: FORGETTING WHAT IS BEHIND AND STRAINING TOWARD WHAT IS AHEAD, I PRESS ON TOWARD THE GOAL TO WIN THE PRIZE FOR WHICH GOD HAS CALLED ME HEAVENWARD IN CHRIST JESUS.

PHILIPPIANS 3:13-14 NIV

"Forgetting" doesn't mean you wake up with amnesia or pretend like nothing ever happened. It means you willfully choose to ignore it. You get to choose whether you will minimize or magnify the experience. You can't pretend like the mistakes, failures, betrayal, or abandonment weren't real, but you can choose wether or not you make it bigger or smaller.

For example, maybe you magnify fear, worry, and anxiety by focusing on imaginary what ifs. To minimize those feelings, you can give your attention to God's Word and His promises, which magnifies His peace and goodness.

Stop choosing to amplify all the awful things that have happened to you, which only causes negative emotions to grow stronger and stronger, and, instead, focus on the good things God has planned for you.

OH, MAGNIFY THE LORD WITH ME, AND LET US EXALT HIS NAME TOGETHER.

PSALM 34:3 KJV

When you magnify an object, the object itself does not become larger. You do not change the actual size of the object. The only thing that changes is your perspective. When you magnify God, He gets bigger and bigger, while your problems and hurts seem to get smaller and smaller.

This means your problems do not determine their size. You do. You determine how big the situation is going to be. So forget those things that are behind, and focus on God's good and perfect plan for your life.

FEEL FREE

7

ACTION

One of my friends is a nutritionist and every time I speak to her she talks to me about eating better. If you're unfamiliar, seeing a nutritionist usually consists of listing everything you have eaten so they can inform you of how terrible all those choices are for your health. It's like going to a confessional for food. I don't need that kind of guilt in my life, so I lie to feel better. My conversation so somewhat like this:

"On Monday I had a sandwich with no mayo or cheese."

"That's good. What kind of bread did you use?"

"Chocolate."

"What kind of sandwich is that?"

"An ice cream sandwich."

"What did you have for dinner?"

"I had a salad."

"What kind of dressing?"

"Ketchup."

"What kind of salad was that?"

"Well, it was a cheeseburger with lettuce, onions, and tomatoes. Technically, the salad was inside of the cheeseburger."

I want to eat healthier, but healthy food doesn't taste good. My nutritionist friend says if you start eating healthier, you will start to crave healthy foods. Your actions can actually change the way you feel about certain foods. This is how the law of action works in our lives.

HAVE I NOT COMMANDED YOU? BE STRONG AND OF GOOD COURAGE; DO NOT BE AFRAID, NOR BE DISMAYED, FOR THE LORD YOUR GOD IS WITH YOU WHEREVER YOU GO."
JOSHUA 1:9

God doesn't tell Joshua to *feel* strong and courageous. He tells him to *be* strong and courageous. God knows sometimes you have to be strong even when you don't feel strong. You can't live your life following your feelings. You have to live your life and let your feelings catch up. That is the law of action.

THE LAW OF ACTION

The law of action means you can act your way into the feelings you desire. Motion creates emotion. Even the word emotion itself is 86% motion. So if you take the right action, you will produce the right feelings.

In life you have two choices: you can let your feelings drive your actions, allowing your emotions to determine how you will respond in any given situation, or you can act on principle regardless of how you feel and do the right thing even when you don't feel like it.

Option number one is a guaranteed way to ruin your life. But when you act on principle and do what is right regardless of feelings, you create the right emotions. Your feelings typically drive your behavior, but your behavior can also drive your feelings. If you choose to do what is right, you will also generate the right feelings.

Let's imagine someone does something that hurts you. You're not just wounded emotionally, but you are angry and your feelings say, "Revenge!" You know how to get back at this person. Everything in you wants to retaliate. Even still, you have a choice to make;you can follow through with the revenge and ultimately end up more hurt, or you can do what is right and forgive that person because that is what Jesus tells us to do.

In this situation, let's say you go with your feelings and take revenge. The action of taking revenge will generate feelings associated with revenge. The anger will get worse and the bitterness will grow. On the other hand, let's say you choose to forgive. As the decision is made, you will start to feel more forgiving. Now, it may not happen instantly, but your feelings will start to change over time. Praying for the person who hurt you will cause your feelings to change even quicker. When you see them in public and choose to treat them with kindness, the way you feel will change. Eventually, you will no longer hold any anger, bitterness or resentment towards them. You can act your way into the feelings you want.

THE COMMON UNDERSTANDING IS THAT TO ACT IN A WAY INCONSISTENT WITH OUR FEELINGS IS FAKE, BUT IGNORING THE LAW OF ACTION MEANS YOU'LL ONLY EXPERIENCE POSITIVE EMOTIONS WHEN THEY ARISE SPONTANEOUSLY.

The problem many people run into is believing that if, "If you have to work at it, it's not genuine." They think if your feelings are authentic, then they should also be automatic. The common understanding is that to act in a way inconsistent with our feelings is fake, but ignoring the law of action means you'll only experience positive emotions when they arise spontaneously. This way of living results in you being at the mercy of how you feel when you wake up each day.

This will cause you to continually forfeit your peace and joy.

Waiting for positive emotions to be triggered by something external is one way to live, but I believe the better way of living is to act your way into the feelings you desire.

ACT YOUR WAY INTO FEELING

Acting your way into feeling is not being fake. You actually do this all the time. Have you ever woke up in the morning and didn't feel like exercising? That is my daily experience, but I force myself to get up and put on my workout clothes. By the time I get in the gym, I still don't have a ton of motivation, but the more I exercise, the more I feel like exercising. Within 15 minutes, I'm glad I got up to work out. If you can do this with exercise, you can do this in any area of your life.

A woman went to see a marriage counselor and said, "I'm so sick of my husband. I'm done. He has become the most rude, lethargic, distant, and emotionally unavailable man. This is not who I married. I want a divorce. Not only do I want a divorce, but I want to hurt him." The counselor said, "I can tell you are really hurting and you can get a divorce, but you will continue to carry this pain with you. You are my client, not him, so I'll tell you what you can do to really hurt him. It's called revenge therapy."

He said, "For the next two months, you are going to act like you are crazy about him. Cook him his favorite meals, go out on dates, encourage and praise him, just like you did when you first got married. Act like you are crazy in love! At the end of two months, drop the hammer and serve him with divorce papers. He won't see it coming, and he'll never be able to trust anyone ever again."

She loved it. She went home, cooked dinner, served him, acted like she was crazy about him. At the end of two months the counselor called and asked, "Are you ready to go forward with the divorce?" She said, "No, the craziest thing happened. He's nuts about me, and I'm in love with him again. It's like we've fallen in love all over again, and we are going on a second honeymoon next week." Seeing the results of his plan play out perfectly the counselor said, "Great. Revenge therapy worked."

Emotions follow motion. First act, then the feelings will come. Hence, if want to change any negative emotion in your life, simply act the way you wish you felt and your feelings will follow.

PART 3

THINK
FREE

FEEL FREE 8

YOUR MIND MATTERS

Harry Houdini was a famed escape artist who issued a challenge everywhere he went. He claimed he could break out of any jail cell in the world. He was always able to follow through on that promise, until one day his stunt didn't quite go as planned.

Houdini entered the jail in his street clothes and the door closed behind him. He pulled a skinny, flexible piece of metal out of his pants and used it to try to pick the lock. Thirty minutes later, he hadn't gotten anywhere. One hour later, still nothing. By this time, he was sweaty and frustrated. Two hours went by, and he still couldn't pick the lock.

Finally, he gave up and collapsed in failure as he leaned up against the door he couldn't unlock. To his surprise, when he leaned against the door, it opened right away because the door had never been locked. He was trying to pick the lock on a door that wasn't even locked. He thought it was locked, so he stayed trapped in a prison when all he had to do was open the door and walk out. The only place the prison door was locked was in his mind, and it kept him from experiencing freedom.[1]

FREEDOM STARTS IN THE MIND

Feeling free starts with your mind. If you don't think you're free, you'll never really feel free. What you think matters more than you think. Many people believe what they think doesn't matter because it's what they do that really matters. While the way you behave is important, it all starts with the way you think.

I've heard it said that it only takes thirty seconds for a thought to become a feeling. If that's true, you have thirty seconds to deal with a thought when it enters your mind. If you take longer to handle the thought, you will have to fight both the thought and the feeling. As we've discussed in the last couple chapters, you can fight feelings, but it takes a lot of work.

Dealing with your thoughts before they become emotions is crucial to feeling free. Your feelings will eventually lead to choices.

Choices when repeated become habits. Habits form your character, and your character determines your destiny. Your feelings, choices, habits and character are all established by your thoughts.

BE CAREFUL HOW YOU THINK; YOUR LIFE IS SHAPED BY YOUR THOUGHTS.
PROVERBS 4:23 GNT

Thoughts shape your life, and it all starts with shaping your feelings first. You cannot think one way and feel another. You can't think negative thoughts and feel positive emotions any more than you can plant apple seeds and expect oranges to grow.

Being joyful follows thinking joyful thoughts. Being peaceful comes from thinking peaceful thoughts. Worry is formed in your mind by thinking worrisome thoughts. Being afraid is a result of thinking fearful thoughts. Emotions are the result of what fills your mind. Thoughts create feelings.

If you contantly think negative thoughts like how everything in your life is horrible, how nobody cares or loves you and how nobody has it as bad as you do, then how do you think you're going to feel? Not good! You can't experience positive emotions with a negative thought life, because your emotions are merely a reflection of your thoughts.

YOU CAN'T EXPERIENCE POSITIVE EMOTIONS WITH A NEGATIVE THOUGHT LIFE, BECAUSE YOUR EMOTIONS ARE MERELY A REFLECTION OF YOUR THOUGHTS

One time, a minister went to preach at another pastor's church and stayed in the pastor's guest bedroom. When he arrived at the pastor's home, he ate dinner and then went to bed because he was exhausted. In the middle of the night, he was suddenly awakened by a rustling noise coming from the corner of the bedroom. He quickly sat up in bed, but he was unable to see clearly since the room was very dark. As his eyes adjusted to the light, he was able to see a large dark image in the corner of the room. It appeared to be moving and was making a strange rustling noise.

The minister was very afraid, thinking a demon had entered the room. He immediately started to pray. After a few minutes of prayer, it stopped moving and the rustling noise ceased, so he went back to sleep. Within a few moments, the strange apparition started to move again and make the strange noise. Again, he started praying and it stopped a few minutes later. This continued all night long, about every twenty minutes or so. He was up all night long in fear praying this figure in the corner would leave.

When the sun started to rise and the first rays of light entered the bedroom, the pastor was able to see clearly. What he had been seeing the entire night wasn't a demon. It was an old raincoat hanging on the coat rack in the corner of the bedroom. The coat would rustle and move as the air conditioning vent blew on it.[2]

Thoughts will determine your feelings even when the things you are thinking about aren't true. Thoughts, even if untrue, still produce real feelings. This is why it's so important to think about the right things.

BE MINDFUL

There are a lot of things that get lost in translation between England and the United States. I'm sure it's annoying for those of you across the ocean to hear what we Americans have done to the Queen's English. Yet, it's just as difficult for Americans to understand the words of those native to England. It goes both ways. For example, across the pond, an apartment is called a flat. An elevator is a lift. A shopping cart at a grocery store is a push trolley. You don't throw garbage in the trash can; it goes in the bin. A diaper is a nappy. Potato chips are crisps and french fries are chips. It's all really confusing.

There is one English phrase I do prefer. In the U.S. we say "watch your head" as a warning you are about to bump your head on something. In England, if there's a low overhang, you'll see a sign that says, "Mind your head"—meaning, be mindful you don't hit your head. I like that phrase because it makes more sense than "Watch your head!" Watching your head is problematic because your eyes happen to be mounted on it. Instead of watching your head, you can be mindful to duck so you don't end up hitting your head.

When it comes to your thoughts, you need to be mindful. Think about what you're thinking about. Next time you feel depressed, audit your thought patterns. This can help you identify the source of your depression. Next time you feel guilty, think about the thoughts that have been running through your head. It will reveal the source of your guilt. When envy leaves you feeling bitter because others have it better, ask yourself, "What have I been mulling over in my mind?" You'll find the source of that emotion. This is why we have to be mindful of our thoughts.

I know this is easier said than done. Sixty-thousand thoughts go through the average person's mind a day, and 80% of those thoughts are negative.[3]

CREDIT CARD

Your mind is like a credit card. Every time a negative thought goes through your mind, it's like a credit card being swiped. "See those people over there? They are probably talking about me. I don't have the right clothes. If only I looked like her, I would be happy. I'm so stupid. I can't do anything right. I can't make it through one day without messing up. If they knew what I am really like, they wouldn't love me. Nobody really likes me." Swipe. Swipe. Swipe.

Every time you believe those thoughts, it's like swiping a credit card, and it will cost you. Credit cards can be dangerous because you don't see the money disappearing from your account but eventually, you will get the bill. This is a bill you have to pay, unlike our national debt, which we are never going to pay back. At the end of 2021, the United States' national debt was just under 29 trillion dollars. Every election cycle, it seems like someone talks about the national debt and how we are going to pay it down. Seriously? We are 29 trillion dollars in debt. We aren't paying anyone back. That was never a part of the plan.

You don't get into 29 trillion dollars worth of debt if you are planning on paying it back. That's the kind of money you take from a loan shark when you think you are going to die in a week. People are always worried about China. We owe China 1.1 trillion dollars and America's in trouble? No, China's in trouble because they lost 1.1 trillion dollars, and we are never going to pay that back.

There are some bills you don't plan on paying back, but when it comes to the bill from your thoughts, that's not an option. You always have to pay. Negative thoughts will cost you your joy, your peace, your hope, and your freedom. When your account hits a negative balance, you're left with worry, depression, shame, hopelessness, and a host of other debilitating emotions. So again, think about what you're thinking about! Your thoughts will cost you, and left unguided, thoughts will cost you your emotional health and freedom.

FOOTNOTES

1. https://sermons.faithlife.com/sermons/26156-houdini's-failed-escape

2. https://www.youtube.com/watch?v=-CwjeSFhi-M

3. https://tlexinstitute.com/how-to-effortlessly-have-more-positive-thoughts/

FEEL FREE 9

CONTROL YOUR THOUGHTS

Have you noticed when you ask what someone does for a living, you sometimes don't get a clear answer? People tend to make up job titles to make their work sound more important than it is. For example, an environmental maintenance officer is actually a garbage man and the Director of Life Enrichment organizes bingo at the senior center. A drain surgeon is a plumber. An eviction technician is nothing more than a bouncer at a club. A transparent-wall maintenance engineer cleans windows, and an underwater ceramic technician washes dishes. The regional director of imports and exports is a drug dealer. Okay, I made that last one up.

CONTROL YOUR THOUGHTS

People embellish job titles to make their work sound more significant; but, we all have an impressive job title already: Director of Neurological Operations. That's just another way of saying it's your job to manage your mind. It's your responsibility to change the way you think. It is a job completely unique to you, a position that cannot be filled by any other person (not even God).

Controlling your thought life isn't a task God will do for you. Over and over again, the Bible tells us to set our minds, focus our thoughts, and to think on positive things. God wouldn't tell you to do something you don't have the power to do, which means you have the power to control your thoughts. It's your responsibility to change the way you think. And if you change the way you think, it will change the way you feel.

The reformer, Martin Luther, had a great way of illustrating your thought life. He said, "You cannot keep birds from flying over your head, but you can keep them from building a nest in your hair." The birds that fly over your head are the random thoughts going through your mind. In the same manner, you have no control over the thoughts that pop up in your mind. They are often authored by the enemy, implanted by others, or come from your own sinful humanity.

THOUGHTS WILL ALWAYS COME AND GO, BUT YOU DETERMINE IF IT GETS TO MAKE A NEST IN YOUR HAIR AND LIVE IN YOUR MIND.

However, keeping thoughts from making a nest in your hair, *is* within the scope of your ability. In other words, you choose what you continue to think about. Thoughts will always come and go, but you determine if they get to make a nest in your hair and live in your mind.

MEDITATION

What you continue to think about over and over again is what the Bible calls meditation. In Chapter 5, we talked about two kinds of thoughts: head thoughts and heart thoughts. Head thoughts are the birds flying over your head. Heart thoughts are the things you continue to think about and meditate on. What you allow your mind to focus on determines your reality and creates your emotions and feelings.

FOR AS HE THINKS IN HIS HEART, SO IS HE.
PROVERBS 23:7

There is only one thing that defines your being, and that is your thought life. Your thoughts define reality and determine your emotions. Looking at your life and seeing circumstances you don't like creates emotions you don't want. Usually, we respond by trying to change our circumstances. "I don't like her, so I'll change her. I don't like my job, so I'll change jobs. I don't like my kids right now, so I'll try to change them. I don't like my spouse, so I'll get a new one." However, changing circumstances to make yourself feel better never works. The reason why it never works is because the problem isn't around you, rather it's inside of you.

Change must start in your thinking before you can experience change in your life. Wherever you go in life, you go there head first. If you change your thinking, you will change your emotions and feelings, which will then change your circumstances. Your thoughts define your reality. If you move up in life, you move up head first. If you move down in life, you go down head first. If you are happy, you are happy in your mind first. If you are sad, you are sad in your mind first. If you are stuck in life, you are stuck in your mind first because your life follows your thoughts. When the mind is unstuck, life will follow suit. Moving your life in the right direction requires moving your mind first.

When you experience negative emotions, don't try to change the emotion. Emotions are a derivative of our thoughts. Nothing changes in your emotions until you change the way you think. If you change your thoughts, your feelings will change.

The starting place for emotional freedom isn't your emotions. It's your mind. Peace in your emotions results from peace in your mind. Joy in your life comes when you think joyful thoughts. Hope will result from thinking positive thoughts about your future. To feel free, you must think free because changing the way you think changes the way you feel.

CHANGE YOUR THINKING

The book of Lamentations was written by Jeremiah when he was a prophet in the nation of Israel. At this time, Israel had turned its back on God and His ways and the people did whatever they felt like doing. The prophet Jeremiah's message to them was "Turn back to God!" The people ignored him and continued to walk away from God. In moving away from God, they also walked away from His protection and blessing. That's when the Babylonians came in and conquered Israel. They destroyed the city of Jerusalem along with God's temple.

Jeremiah's world as he knew it was over. Lamentations is Jeremiah lamenting over the destruction and loss the Israelites had suffered. In Lamentations 3:1-20, Jeremiah describes how he feels by saying, "I feel like I'm walking in darkness...like my bones have been crushed...bitterness and hardships surround me...I feel trapped in prison that I can't escape...like I'm being weighed down with heavy chains...like my heart has been pierced with an arrow...I have no peace, no comfort, no joy, no hope..."

WHEREVER YOU GO IN LIFE, YOU GO THERE HEAD FIRST.

Jeremiah is definitely in his feels. He's in a very dark place emotionally. What he is describing is textbook depression. But notice how he gets himself out of this place of depression and hopelessness:

"YET THIS I CALL TO MIND AND THEREFORE I HAVE HOPE: BECAUSE OF THE

LORD'S GREAT LOVE WE ARE NOT CONSUMED, FOR HIS COMPASSIONS NEVER FAIL.THEY ARE NEW EVERY MORNING; GREAT IS YOUR FAITHFULNESS."
LAMENTATIONS 3:21-23 NIV

Jeremiah was thinking about all the terrible things that could have been avoided. He was thinking of all the things he lost. But then he started recalling the goodness of God. He remembered God's love and mercy. He remembered God's faithfulness. Jeremiah focused on God's unfailing, relentless love. It was this change in his thinking that brought him out of the pit of depression and despair and into freedom. When his thinking changed, his emotions changed. You can never change the way you feel until you change the way you think. This change in your thinking is what the Bible calls renewing your mind.

RENEW YOUR MIND

THEREFORE, I URGE YOU, BROTHERS AND SISTERS, IN VIEW OF GOD'S MERCY, TO OFFER YOUR BODIES AS A LIVING SACRIFICE, HOLY AND PLEASING TO GOD—THIS IS YOUR TRUE AND PROPER WORSHIP. AND DO NOT BE CONFORMED TO THIS WORLD, BUT BE TRANSFORMED BY THE RENEWING OF YOUR MIND, THAT YOU MAY PROVE WHAT IS THAT GOOD AND ACCEPTABLE AND PERFECT WILL OF GOD.
ROMANS 12:1 NIV

Transformation doesn't happen by willpower, self effort, or trying harder. Transformation takes place in your life when you change your mind. You can't feel free by trying to change your emotions; you feel free by changing your mind. Nothing changes in your life until you change the way you think. You may want God to change your circumstances, or take away all your problems, or even make you feel differently, but God is more interested in changing your mind.

Even if God removed all of your problems and negative emotions, it would be a matter of time before you'd find yourself in the same place with the same feelings. For this reason, God desires to change your mind more than your circumstances or emotions.

When your mind is renewed, your emotions take care of themselves. The word renew means 'to renovate.'[1] When you renovate a house, you tear out the old carpet to put in hardwood floors. You knock down walls to create a more open concept. You tear out the old cabinets and replace them with new ones.

When you renovate a house, you take out the old and replace it with something new. That is what it means to renew your mind. It means do away with the old, outdated, faulty thinking, and replace it with God's thoughts God's truth, and God's promises. In the next chapter, we will look at how to practically renew your mind so you can feel free.

FOOTNOTES

1. https://www.vocabulary.com/dictionary/renovate

FEEL FREE

10

TAKING THOUGHTS CAPTIVE

In brute strength, elephants are one of the strongest animals on the earth. African elephants can weigh over 6 tons and they can carry up to 9 tons. To put it in perspective, that's about the weight of 130 adult humans. In certain parts of Asia, farmers still use elephants to do much of their heavy labor. Elephants pull stumps and trees out of the ground, haul logs, and carry heavy loads.

But do you know how they keep elephants from just walking off whenever they want? The owners take a piece of rope and tie it to a wooden post. They then tie the piece of rope to the elephant's right hind leg, and that's it.

The elephant could tear the rope and the entire wooden post out of the ground with little effort! Yet, the rope and wooden post actually keep the elephant from wandering off. When an elephant is still a baby, the owner shackles him to a large tree with a heavy chain around his right hind leg.

For days and weeks, the young elephant will strain and pull trying to break free. Eventually, he gives up struggling and accepts the idea that he can't go anywhere when something is around his right hind leg. Soon, the owner can replace the tree with a little wooden post and the chain with a piece of rope. Now, once the elephant feels any resistance, he stops pulling.

The powerful giant has been conditioned by his prior experience to think when something is around his leg, he's stuck. In reality, the only place he's stuck is in his mind. Whenever you get stuck in life, it's because you are stuck in your mind. In order to move forward, your thinking must be transformed. As we learned int he last chapter, the process of changing the way you think is what the Bible calls renewing the mind (Romans 12:1-2). Renewing the mind starts with taking every thought captive.

> FOR THOUGH WE LIVE IN THE WORLD, WE DO NOT WAGE WAR AS THE WORLD DOES. THE WEAPONS WE FIGHT WITH ARE NOT THE WEAPONS OF THE WORLD. ON THE CONTRARY, THEY HAVE DIVINE POWER TO DEMOLISH STRONGHOLDS. WE DEMOLISH ARGUMENTS AND EVERY PRETENSION THAT SETS ITSELF UP AGAINST THE KNOWLEDGE OF GOD, AND WE TAKE CAPTIVE EVERY THOUGHT TO MAKE IT OBEDIENT TO CHRIST.
>
> 2 CORINTHIANS 10:3-5 NIV

Depression, fear, anxiety, discouragement, anger, and lust aren't behavior problems. They are thought problems. The only way to find victory over these emotions is to take every thought captive and make it obedient to Jesus Christ.

STRONGHOLDS

First we take every thought captive by demolishing strongholds. Some think strongholds are demonic principalities and powers in the unseen realm. These strongholds, however, aren't in the spiritual realm. They are between your ears. A stronghold is a lie you believe to be true.

While children are growing up, parents tell all kinds of lies. They used to say sitting too close to the TV would ruin your eyesight. Now, we have screens 6 inches from our face all the time and it hasn't affected our eyesight. I was told if I peed in the pool, there was a special dye that would turn my pee red and everyone would know I peed in the pool. Were you ever told anything like that? How about some of these: If you swallow gum, it will stay in your stomach for seven years. Drinking coffee stunts your growth. Touching a frog will give you warts. Cracking your knuckles causes arthritis. If you make a funny face, it will get stuck that way. Family pets go to live on the farm where they have room to run and play forever. They're all lies!

Most of those lies probably didn't have a huge impact on who you are today. But the lies you believe about God, others, and yourself can become strongholds controlling your behavior. We all have feelings we want to resist, but don't fight the feeling. Instead, fight the lie! When the lie is replaced with truth, the negative emotion has no place to live. You have to address the lie causing the feeling.

Take anger and resentment, for example. If you have anger and resentment towards someone, it's based on the lie that God is not a vindicator. It's based on the lie that God won't handle those who harmed you, or if God is going to handle them, he's taking too long to do it. But God says don't take revenge because vengeance is mine (Romans 12:19). God is a vindicator, and He will handle those who hurt you. He just might not do it the way you would do it. If it was up to us, we would just wipe them out!

God doesn't wipe out our enemies though. He keeps them around so they can watch you succeed. Why? Because there is nothing worse than wanting someone to fail and having to watch them succeed. God punishes your enemies by making the same people who made you cry watch you smile, and they are watching. They might not be liking your pictures on social media, but they're on your page. When you know the truth that God is a vindicator, anger and resentment have no place. You can demolish strongholds by replacing lies with the truth of God's Word.

> **WHEN THE LIE IS REPLACED WITH TRUTH, THE NEGATIVE EMOTION HAS NO PLACE TO LIVE.**

ARGUMENTS AND PRETENSIONS

Next, 2 Corinthians says you are to demolish arguments. An argument is any thought that comes into your mind that tries to contradict God's Word.

God's Word says, He wants to bless you.

You may think, "God wants to bless others, but He doesn't want to bless me."

God's Word says, you are loved.

You think, "God can't love me because of what I have done."

God's Word also says, you have been given gifts.

You may think, "I don't have any gifts."

Instead of accepting God's Word as truth, we tend to argue with it. WE allow contradicting thoughts to push out God's Word. But by refusing to allow anything to contradict what God has said, you can demolish arguments.

We also have to demolish pretensions. Other translations call pretensions "high things that exalt themselves above the knowledge of God." Pretensions are when you allow your assumptions to have the highest place in your life. This inner dialogue has a familiar rhythm to it.

I know God's Word says… but I think…

I know Scripture says 'Don't...' but I think it's okay.

I know the Bible says... but God's Word is an archaic book, and I don't think I have to do that any more.

By allowing our assumptions and preferences to supersede what God has said, we live out of your pretensions and not the reality of God's truth.

We are called to demolish strongholds, arguments, and every pretension that sets itself up against the knowledge of God. You do that by taking captive every thought not lining up with God's Word. Strongholds, arguments, pretensions, and negative thoughts are like weeds in your mind. The weeds need to be continually pulled out and uprooted whenever you encounter them.

PULLING WEEDS

As a kid, one of the things I would do to make money was pull weeds in my grandmother's backyard. She had this huge backyard, but she didn't have grass. Her backyard would get overrun with weeds, and I would go over there a pull up every single weed. But do you know what happens when dirt is left with no grass to occupy it? The weeds come right back. I'd have to come back a couple months later and pull up the weeds all over again. I had to continually pull

> **STRONGHOLDS, ARGUMENTS, PRETENSIONS, AND NEGATIVE THOUGHTS ARE LIKE WEEDS IN YOUR MIND.**

weeds because she never planted anything good in the backyard. If she would have planted grass, I wouldn't have had to continually pull weeds every couple of months.

Renewing your mind involves uprooting and replacing negative thoughts. It's not enough to just uproot distorted thought patterns. You have to replace them with good thoughts and with healthy thought patterns. If not, you will continually be pulling up the same weeds over and over again. By planting the seed of God's Word into your heart and mind, you can grow healthy, life-giving thought patterns. Next, we will look at practical ways you can plant God's Word in your heart and mind.

FEEL FREE
11

PLANTING THE WORD

As you have already learned, eating healthy is not something I enjoy in the least. I blame my continual struggle on the education system and Pizza Hut. When I was in school, they had this program called “Book It” to solve the literacy problem in America. “Book It” provided kids with a personal pan pizza if they read four books (or if they lied and told their teacher they read four books). It was great. You got pizza for doing homework (or lying about doing homework). I’m sure you can guess how someone clever might have taken advantage of that brilliant program.

Most likely "Book It" would not be an acceptable solution for today's education system. People have become much more health conscious. I was eating at a restaurant and the waiter said, "I'm sorry we spilt cheese on your fries." Why did he apologize? It's not poison. It's cheese! That's a good thing. That's like spilling frosting on a cake or spilling sunshine on a cloudy day. That's a good thing not a mistake.

I struggle with eating healthy because let's be honest healthy food just doesn't taste good. One time I wanted to eat healthy so I bought rice cakes. I bought them because the package had the word cake on it, but when I took a bite, I didn't think of cake at all. It tasted more like a packing peanut than cake. This is why I struggle when it comes to eating healthy. Healthy food doesn't taste good and junk food tastes great.

A friend of mine gave me a strategy to move towards healthier eating. The strategy involved getting rid of all the junk food in my house and filling my fridge will healthy food. This way when I want a snack, my only options are healthy food. By filling up on healthy foods, it's easier to say no to junk food. This doesn't just apply to having healthy dietary habits. It is exactly how you can begin to transform your mind. Filling your mind with God's Word makes it easier to stop negative thoughts from taking root.

POWER OF THE WORD

"RECEIVE WITH MEEKNESS THE ENGRAFTED WORD, WHICH IS ABLE TO

SAVE YOUR SOULS."
JAMES 1:21 KJV

God's Word has the power to change your soul, which is comprised of your mind, will, and emotions. However the Word won't change you until it's grafted into your heart and mind. By receiving God's Word and grafting it into your heart, it has the power to change the way you think. In turn, the truth in your heart, changes your emotions.

What does this look like practically?

If you are afraid, fill your mind with 2 Timothy 1:7. "God has not given me a spirit of fear but of power and love and a sound mind."

If you experience temptation, feed your thoughts with 1 Corinthians 10:13. "No temptation has taken me but such as is common to man but God is faithful who will not allow me to be tempted beyond what I am able but will with the temptation also make a way of escape."

If you are feeling condemned, remind your heart of 2 Corinthians 5:21. "God made Jesus to be sin for me that I can become the righteousness of God."

If you are worried about not having enough money, meditate on Philippians 4:19 "My God shall supply all my needs according to his riches in glory by Christ Jesus."

PLANTING THE WORD

If you feel stressed because you have big decisions to make, set your thoughts on Proverbs 3:5-6. "Trust in the Lord with all my heart and lean not on my own understanding; in all my ways submit to him, and he will make my paths straight."

If you're discouraged because you just experienced a setback, anchor your thoughts with Romans 8:28. "God works all things together for good."

Don't focus on what you don't want to think about; instead, direct your thoughts on God's Word and God's promises. I've found the best way to do this is through reciting Scripture and worship

> "LET THE WORD OF CHRIST DWELL IN YOU RICHLY IN ALL WISDOM, TEACHING AND ADMONISHING ONE ANOTHER IN PSALMS AND HYMNS AND SPIRITUAL SONGS, SINGING WITH GRACE IN YOUR HEARTS TO THE LORD."
> COLOSSIANS 3:16 NIV

Meditating on Scripture and engaging in worship can put your mind and heart into airplane mode, making it impervious to low level thinking. These habits can curb the negative thoughts continually bombarding your mind. Trying to stop thinking about something will only cause it to stick in your mind more. For example, don't think about a pink elephant. What did you just do? You thought about a pink elephant.

The only way not to think about pink elephants is to think about something else instead. You have to feed your mind with positive thoughts in order to replace negative ones.

God says, "You are a new creation in Christ... You are loved ... You are chosen... You are accepted...You are complete in Christ.... You are a child of God... You are God's masterpiece...You are fearfully and wonderfully made.... You were created with a purpose and destiny."

THE MORE YOU PLANT GOD'S WORD AND WHAT HE SAYS ABOUT YOU INTO YOUR HEART AND MIND, THE LESS ROOM THERE WILL BE FOR WEEDS TO SPRING UP.

The more you plant God's Word and what He says about you into your heart and mind, the less room there will be for weeds to spring up. As you can see, it's not enough to just read God's Word. You have to have it grafted into your heart and mind. Once the graft takes place, it produces a harvest of love, joy, peace, patience, kindness, goodness, faithfulness, gentleness, and self control (Galatians 5:22-23).

FEEL FREE 12

TALK TO YOURSELF

There are a lot of differences between men and women.

The average man has four items in his bathroom. A tooth brush, a razor, a bar of soap, and a towel from the Holiday Inn.

The average number of items in a typical woman's bathroom is 437. The average man can only identify four of those items.

Men will pay $20 for a $10 item they really want. Women will pay $10 for a $20 item they don't want.

A woman has the last word in any argument and anything a man says after that is the beginning of a new argument.

Women love cats. Men say they love cats, but when women aren't looking, they kick cats.

What's the difference between women and terrorists? Terrorists negotiate. What's the difference between men and government bonds? Bond's mature.

A woman knows all about her children. She knows about their dentist appointments, best friends, favorite foods, secret fears, hopes, and dreams. A man is vaguely aware of short people living in the house.

WHEN YOUR THOUGHTS START TO SPIRAL DOWNWARDS, YOU NEED TO SPEAK THE WORD OR GOD.

I've heard it said the average woman uses 20,000 words a day, while the average man uses 7,000 words a day.

I'm not sure whether that last statement is fact or fiction, but I do know regardless of how much you talk to others, you need to make sure you talk to yourself. You have to confess God's Word over your life because speaking God's Word from your mouth can change your mind. When your thoughts are spiraling in the wrong direction, you can't interrupt a thought with thought. You interrupt thoughts with words.

INTERRUPTING THOUGHTS

When teaching on this subject, I'll have the audience count to

10 in their minds. While they are counting in their heads, I'll have them say their name aloud. As soon as they say their name, they stop counting in their heads. Go ahead. You can try it. I'll wait right here...

See, what is coming out of your mouth interrupts what was going on in your minds. You can't think one thing while saying something else. What you say will disrupt whatever you are thinking. When your thoughts start to spiral downwards, you need to speak the Word of God.

For instance, if the thought comes, "I am always going to be poor." You say, "My God will supply all of my needs according to his riches in glory" (Philippians 4:19). If the thought comes, "I'll always be an addict." You say, "I can do all things through Christ who gives me strength" (Philippians 4:13). If the thought comes, "I'll never recover from this." You say, "God works all things together for good in my life"(Romans 8:28). When you open your mouth and speak the Word of God, you can interrupt negative thoughts before they become negative emotions. This is what Jesus did when He was tempted by the devil.

THEN JESUS WAS LED BY THE SPIRIT INTO THE WILDERNESS TO BE TEMPTED BY THE DEVIL. AFTER FASTING FORTY DAYS AND FORTY NIGHTS, HE WAS HUNGRY. DURING THAT TIME THE DEVIL CAME AND SAID TO HIM, "IF YOU ARE THE SON OF GOD, TELL THESE STONES TO BECOME LOAVES OF BREAD."
MATTHEW 4:1-3 NLT

Many theologians don't believe this was a physical appearance of Satan. They believe this temptation took place in Jesus' mind. It's believed these were thoughts the enemy was putting into the mind of Jesus. Now, I'm not sure whether or not that's true, but it is exactly how the enemy tempts you. The enemy puts thoughts in your mind! Look at how Jesus responded when He was tempted:

BUT JESUS TOLD HIM, "NO! THE SCRIPTURES SAY, 'PEOPLE DO NOT LIVE BY BREAD ALONE, BUT BY EVERY WORD THAT COMES FROM THE MOUTH OF GOD.'"
MATTHEW 4:4 NLT

Jesus responded by speaking the Word of God. Jesus was tempted two more times in Matthew 4, and He responded to every temptation the exact same way. He spoke the Word of God. Every time the devil talked to Jesus, Jesus talked back. If you are going to win the battle in your mind, you have to talk to yourself. Every time the enemy puts a negative thought in your mind, you need to talk back! Your mood will be determined by who you let have the last word.

WHEN YOU OPEN YOUR MOUTH AND SPEAK THE WORD OF GOD, YOU CAN INTERRUPT NEGATIVE THOUGHTS BEFORE THEY BECOME NEGATIVE EMOTIONS.

Allowing the devil to have the last word will be reflected by your mood. When you allow God to have the last word, you will feel it. When the enemy talks to you, you'd better open your mouth and talk back, or he will talk you out of your joy. He'll talk you out of your peace. He'll talk you out of your hope.

But here is the good news: even if you've lost your joy, your peace, and your hope, you can get it back. Because words not only interrupt thoughts before they become emotions, but they have the power to change the way you feel. If you change your words, your feelings will follow.

FEELINGS FOLLOW WORDS

In chapter nine, we looked at the prophet Jeremiah experiencing depression. We saw how he pulled himself out of the pit of depression by changing his thoughts.

"THIS I RECALL TO MY MIND, THEREFORE I HAVE HOPE. THROUGH THE LORD'S MERCIES WE ARE NOT CONSUMED, BECAUSE HIS COMPASSIONS FAIL NOT. THEY ARE NEW EVERY MORNING; GREAT IS YOUR FAITHFULNESS."
LAMENTATIONS 3:21-23

This verse in Lamentations shows how this change in Jeremiah's thinking also changed his emotions. Jeremiah didn't stop there.

I SAY TO MYSELF, "THE LORD IS MY INHERITANCE; THEREFORE, I WILL HOPE IN HIM!." THE LORD IS GOOD TO THOSE WHOSE HOPE IS IN HIM, TO THE ONE WHO SEEKS HIM; IT IS GOOD TO WAIT PATIENTLY FOR THE SALVATION OF THE LORD."
LAMENTATIONS 3:24-26 NIV

He didn't just change his thoughts. He changed his words. Jeremiah talked to himself. He said, "The Lord is my inheritance. I WILL

HOPE in Him! The Lord is good to those who hope in Him!" When he was feeling hopeless, he declared hope. When everything around him was bad, he declared the goodness of God. He spoke the opposite of what he was feeling.

LET THE WEAK SAY, 'I AM STRONG.'
JOEL 3:10

Notice Joel 3:10 doesn't say, "let the weak talk about their weakness" or "Let the weak complain about their weakness." No, 'Let the weak say, 'I am strong.' " Let the weak say exactly the opposite of how they feel. In other words, don't talk about the way you are. Talk about the way you want to be.

This verse could also say: Let the discouraged say, "I have courage." Let the defeated say, "I have victory." Let the stressed say, "I have peace." Let the broke say, "I have money!" Let the depressed say, "I have joy." We have to speak the opposite of what we are feeling and experiencing. We have to proclaim the change we want to see in our lives. And there is nothing more powerful than proclaiming God's Word.

If you want to shift your emotions and change your feelings, you need to talk to yourself. You need to speak the Word of God over your life.

PART 4

STAY FREE

FEEL FREE 13

AUDIT YOUR INTAKE

Exposure is a powerful force. What you think about and what you eventually feel is often a result of what you've been exposed to. That's why an audit of the things you expose your mind to on a regular basis is a good idea to maintain a healthy thought life. Your mind is like a sponge. If you dip a sponge in blue water and squeeze it, blue water will come out. If you dip the sponge in red water and squeeze it, red water will come out. Since the mind is a sponge, it acts on what it soaks up. When it's squeezed, the only possible thing that can come out is what it was already in contact with. What comes out of your mind is determined by what you put in. If junk goes in, the only thing that can come out is junk. It's impossible to avoid this.

> MY SON, GIVE ATTENTION TO MY WORDS; INCLINE YOUR EAR TO MY SAYINGS. DO NOT LET THEM DEPART FROM YOUR EYES; KEEP THEM IN THE MIDST OF YOUR HEART; FOR THEY ARE LIFE TO THOSE WHO FIND THEM, AND HEALTH TO ALL THEIR FLESH. KEEP YOUR HEART WITH ALL DILIGENCE, FOR OUT OF IT SPRING THE ISSUES OF LIFE. PUT AWAY FROM YOU A DECEITFUL MOUTH, AND PUT PERVERSE LIPS FAR FROM YOU. LET YOUR EYES LOOK STRAIGHT AHEAD, AND YOUR EYELIDS LOOK RIGHT BEFORE YOU.
> PROVERBS 4:20-25

Whatever you put in will eventually come out. This is why Scripture tells us to give careful attention to what we hear and what we see. When we are aware of this dynamic, we can mitigate the damage of negative exposures. The problem is most people never audit their intake. If you passively ingest everything culture shovels at you, you will gradually be conformed to this world. You will miss out on the renewed mind God wants for you. Renewing your mind requires a deliberate choice to put good things in and keep bad things out.

It's important to know how much of who or what we can intake. There are some people we can only handle in small doses. We can't be around them for extended periods of time without them affecting our minds and our mood. Let's look at some examples.

If you are bent towards negativity when you experience hardships, you need to avoid pessimistic people in those moments. It doesn't mean you need to put them out of your life completely; you just might need to put them in another place.

If you tend to get angry, there are certain people you may need to avoid. There will be those who calm you down and there are others who only make you feel justified in your resentment. If you're angry, there are people you shouldn't talk to. It doesn't mean you never talk to them; you just have to be selective on when you talk to them.

RENEWING YOUR MIND REQUIRES A DELIBERATE CHOICE TO PUT GOOD THINGS IN AND KEEP BAD THINGS OUT.

If you're spending more time watching the news than consuming God's Word and other encouraging spiritual books or podcasts, then don't be surprised when you are fearful, anxious, and discouraged all the time. The news is filled with negativity. Even though there are positive things happening in the world every single day, those things don't make the news. Only the terrible stuff makes the news. Even the weather reports lean towards the negative. They say, "There's a 20% chance of rain" not "there's an 80% chance of sunshine." The news and weather reports always highlight the negative. If your intake of news is too high, your outlook will be negative.

I can always tell which people who watch too much news because they always talk about how bad things are getting in the world. They say, "The world is getting so violent." No, it's actually getting better.

Just go to the book of Genesis when there were only four people on the earth. One couple had two boys. They had the whole world to themselves and one said, "This world isn't big enough for the two of us." Cain killed Abel. The third person on the planet killed the fourth person on the planet. We couldn't even make it to 5 people before someone got murdered.

Cain killed 25% of the world's population. That's more than Stalin, Hitler, and Genghis Khan combined. Cain killed one-third of the people he knew.

After Abel died, one-third of the people alive were murderers. One-third of people in prison aren't even murderers. Alcatraz was safer than the world the book of Genesis describes. You thought Bagdad and Fallujah were tough; try downtown Eden after the sun goes down.

The world has always been violent. There is no such thing as the good ole days. There was only one good day. Actually, it was half a day. Adam and Eve were naked, alone in paradise, and then lunch came around. People got hungry, apples were eaten, and things went downhill from there. The world is actually getting better, but you wouldn't know it from watching the news.

God's kingdom is spreading across the earth. The more it spreads, the more this world begins to line up with everything righteous and just. There is so much good in our world, but it's impossible to feel good about the world if you continually feed on everything that is wrong. There isn't a lot to be gained from watching the news other than an understanding of current events. We need to evaluate how much bad news we can consume before it starts to take a toll on us. We need to make sure we are taking in more good than bad. Consume more beneficial things than worthless things.

FOCUS ON THE GOOD

Focusing on what is good in the world and our own lives isn't an easy thing to do. Psychologists have discovered the human brain captures negative experiences five times more than positive ones. Neuroplasticity is how your brain captures and catalogs information so you can find it and retrieve it later. Like Google, your brain captures and catalogs information so you can find it later. Only our brain captures and catalogs negative experiences five times more than positive ones. You must retrain your brain to focus on the positive. That is exactly what Philippians 4:8 tells us.

FINALLY, BROTHERS AND SISTERS, WHATEVER IS TRUE, WHATEVER IS NOBLE, WHATEVER IS RIGHT, WHATEVER IS PURE, WHATEVER IS LOVELY, WHATEVER IS ADMIRABLE—IF ANYTHING IS EXCELLENT OR PRAISEWORTHY—THINK ABOUT SUCH THINGS.
PHILIPPIANS 4:8 NIV

In the book "Extreme Ownership: How US Navy SEALs Lead and Win," the authors, two former Navy SEALs, talk about how no matter what happens to them, no matter what situation they find themselves in, their response is always, "Good times." Regardless of how unexpected, inopportune, or inconvenient the task in front of them, they always have the same response. That response puts them in the proper frame of mind to stay strong. It increases their effectiveness.

In essence, they are taking a negative situation and seeing it from a different perspective. Psychologists call this tactic "cognitive restructuring." Because whatever you look for, you will find. If you focus on it, you'll find it. It's called the frequency illusion. Once something has been noticed, then every instance is noticed, leading to the belief it has a high frequency of occurrence.[2]

There are two psychological processes that cause the frequency illusion:selective attention and confirmation bias. We've all experienced this before. For example before you buy a car, you get online and do a little research on the car. Let's say it's a Honda Civic. You read all about it. You spend time looking at pictures of Honda Civics. When you get in your car to drive to work, you suddenly see Honda Civics everywhere. You may start to think, "I guess I really need a Honda Civic because they are everywhere. They must be great cars." There weren't more Honda Civics than normal on the road, but selective attention causes you to notice them more. Then confirmation bias kicks in. Your brain notices that you paid attention to it, so it looks for it even more. Now, you are in the frequency illusion.

The frequency illusion isn't bad when it comes to shopping for a new car, but when it comes to negativity, it's a problem. If we look for the bad in every situation, we will find the bad in every situation, which, in turn, causes us to look for it far more. It's a vicious cycle. That's why there are some people that can find the bad in every good situation. Regardless of how good things are, they have something to complain about. They have trained their brain to find the bad.

Bad news can be subversive, but we can train our brains to look for the good. When we become intentional about searching for good, you will find good. This will cause our subconscious mind to look for more good. Before we know it, you'll be able to see the good even when life is bad. Some people might say, "Well, that's just positive thinking." I don't believe in positive thinking as the end in and of itself. I believe in positive thinking as a response to God. Positive thinking is the right response to God's promises. This is what David, a Navy SEAL of the Old Testament, did when facing difficult circumstances.

I WOULD HAVE LOST HEART, UNLESS I HAD BELIEVED THAT I WOULD SEE THE GOODNESS OF THE LORD IN THE LAND OF THE LIVING.
PSALM 27:13

David could have lost heart. He could have given up and gone into depression, but instead, he chose to focus on the goodness of God. It was focusing on God's goodness when life was bad that allowed him to move forward. In faith, he believed God would come through and work all things together for good.

This is also what allowed Joseph to remain confident and expectant. His brothers sold him into slavery. His boss's wife made false sexual allegations against him that put him in jail. The people he helped broke their promises, but Joseph always held onto hope. He trusted God would work all things together for good.

We see this in the end of Joseph's story. When he saw his brothers again, he said, "You meant evil against me, but God meant it for good" (Genesis 50:20). This is more than just positive thinking. It's more than putting out good vibes into the universe and hoping good things will come your way. It's positive thinking in response to God's promise to work all things together for good. So no matter how bad things get, you can always focus on the good.

FOOTNOTES

1. https://www.verywellmind.com/negative-bias-4589618

2. *https://news.ucdenver.edu/what-is-the-frequency-illusion/*

FEEL FREE

15

PREPARING YOUR MIND

Finding freedom from destructive emotions is a start, but it's not enough to get free. We have to live free. Seventy-six percent of people released from prison return within 5 years of being released.[1] Many inmates know how to behave in prison to get free, but they don't know how to live free, so they end up right back in bondage.

Freedom is better but not always easier. Because we can grow accustomed to living in bondage, walking in freedom can be difficult. It requires us to develop new habits, new rhythms, new patterns, and new relationships.

SO JESUS WAS SAYING TO THE JEWS WHO HAD BELIEVED HIM, "IF YOU ABIDE IN MY WORD [CONTINUALLY OBEYING MY TEACHINGS AND LIVING IN ACCORDANCE WITH THEM, THEN] YOU ARE TRULY MY DISCIPLES. AND YOU WILL KNOW THE TRUTH, AND THE TRUTH WILL SET YOU FREE."
JOHN 8:31-31 AMP

Holding fast to Jesus' teachings is essential to living free. We must live out His Word and His principles. The more we devote ourselves to the way of Jesus, the more freedom we will experience in our emotions. Negative emotions will never be completely gone. They will return to enslave us again and again. Harsh feelings will always seek to control us, but walking in the way of Jesus will keep those emotions in check.

JACK IN THE BOX

It's kind of like a jack-in-the-box. If you start winding it up, it's only a matter of time before Jack comes out. We all have a Jack in our box. Jack is what the New Testament calls the old man, or our flesh, and some translations call it our sin nature. It's the nature of sin that is not evicted when we become believers. It stays with you and even when it's not active, it's present.

All it takes is for someone or something to wind us up, and Jack will come out. We might not be experiencing negative emotions at the moment, but it doesn't mean they're not lurking beneath the surface. Our jack-in-the-box never goes away completely. In other words, destructive emotions that want to hijack our lives never go away permanently. They will always try to come back.

The hope is the more we practice the principles of Scripture, the longer it takes for Jack to come out! The more emotionally healthy we are, the less negative emotions will set us off. That is the goal. We will never reach emotional perfection, but we can achieve emotional health. We can get to a place where Jack isn't always popping out of the box and sabotaging our success. This is made possible when we devote ourselves to living out the ways of Jesus.

EXAMPLE OF JESUS

To see how you can keep your jack-in-the-box in check, we are going to look at the example of Jesus in Mark 14. Here, Jesus is in the Garden of Gethsemane mere hours before He goes to the cross. Gethsemane is known as the place of crushing because it was filled with olive trees. The only way to get oil out of olives is to crush them. What this place represented physically is what Jesus experienced emotionally. In Gethsemane, Jesus was under extreme emotional stress and pressure. In fact, Jesus was under such emotional pressure that He was sweating drops of blood.

THE MORE WE DEVOTE OURSELVES TO THE WAY OF JESUS, THE MORE FREEDOM WE WILL EXPERIENCE IN OUR EMOTIONS.

What Jesus experienced in that moment is a condition called Hematidrosis. The capillary blood vessels which feed the sweat glands had ruptured, causing them to exude blood. It only happens under extreme stress and pressure.[2] Jesus is overwhelmed with negative emotions, and we get a glimpse of how Jesus dealt with these emotions.

> THEY WENT TO A PLACE CALLED GETHSEMANE, AND JESUS SAID TO HIS DISCIPLES, "SIT HERE WHILE I PRAY." HE TOOK PETER, JAMES AND JOHN ALONG WITH HIM, AND HE BEGAN TO BE DEEPLY DISTRESSED AND TROUBLED. "MY SOUL IS OVERWHELMED WITH SORROW TO THE POINT OF DEATH," HE SAID TO THEM. "STAY HERE AND KEEP WATCH." GOING A LITTLE FARTHER, HE FELL TO THE GROUND AND PRAYED THAT IF POSSIBLE THE HOUR MIGHT PASS FROM HIM. "ABBA, FATHER," HE SAID, "EVERYTHING IS POSSIBLE FOR YOU. TAKE THIS CUP FROM ME. YET NOT WHAT I WILL, BUT WHAT YOU WILL."
>
> MARK 14:32-36 NIV

When Jesus was distressed, troubled, and overwhelmed with sorrow to the point of death, He first went to God in prayer. Many people treat prayer as a last resort. After exhausting every other option, they turn to God. They say, "Well, all we can do now is pray." To them, prayer is the "break glass in case of emergency" kind of solution. People pull prayer out only when there is a crisis. It's the last thing they do when confronted with a problem, but prayer should to be our first response.

When we find ourselves depressed, anxious, unsure of what to do, or collapsing under the pressure, the first thing we should do is go to God in prayer. Notice Jesus didn't post a Facebook status asking for prayer. Jesus said, "Sit here while I pray." We can't delegate our prayer life to someone else. Other people can go to God with you, but they can't go for you. It's our responsibility to go to God in prayer.

STARTING YOUR DAY

If prayer is going to be our first response, it also needs to be the first thing we do in the morning. I know some of you are thinking "I don't even believe in God until I've had three cups of coffee." I understand, but morning prayer time sets the tone for what you do the rest of the day. Jesus developed a habit of spending time each morning in prayer. If Jesus needed to start his day in prayer, then how much more do we?

"NOW IN THE MORNING, HAVING RISEN A LONG WHILE BEFORE DAYLIGHT, HE (JESUS) WENT OUT AND DEPARTED TO A SOLITARY PLACE; AND THERE HE PRAYED."
MARK 1:35

John Bargh, a social psychologist at Yale University, has been experimenting on unsuspecting college students for years. One of the things his research focuses on is what he calls priming.[3] When you paint a wall, you use primer first and then paint over it. You never see the primer again. You only see the paint, but the primer actually makes a difference in what you can see. What John Bargh has discovered is that our brains, without ever realizing it, get primed everyday, in this same way.

One of the many studies he performed was a scrambled sentence test. In this experiment, there were two different groups of students with two different tests. The students were told to simply group the words given to them into complete sentences. The key difference was that one group had rude words sprinkled throughout their test, while the other group had polite words like respectful, considerate, kind. Both groups took the test. When they were done, they were told to go down the hallway to the professor's office to get their next assignment. An actor was strategically placed with the professor. Upon entering the office, the actor and the professor were engaged in a conversation.

The goal of the study was to see how long it took the students to interrupt the conversation for their purposes. The students who were primed with rude words interrupted, on average, after 5 minutes. While 82% of the students who were primed with kind words never interrupted at all. They just stood there endlessly waiting for the conversation to end. The students never consciously picked up on the word trend in the test, but their brains were still being primed subconsciously. It affected their behavior without them even realizing it.

> OTHER PEOPLE CAN GO TO GOD WITH YOU IN PRAYER, BUT THEY CAN'T GO FOR YOU.

Your thoughts and behaviors in this moment are influenced by what you were thinking about minutes or hours ago. This is especially true of what you do first thing in the morning. Priming your mind with prayer, the Word of God, and worship in the morning sets the tone for the rest of the day. The sooner you engage in these practices the greater the impact they have on the rest of your day even if you don't realize it. The time you spend in prayer in the morning is the primer helping you live like Jesus throughout the day.

Most people don't start their day in prayer. Most of us start our day by rolling over in bed and grabbing our phones. You can tell how old a person is by how far they sleep from their cell phone. If you are under the age of twenty, you probably sleep with it in your hand or under your pillow. If you are in twenties, it's usually within arm's reach at all times. If you are over thirty, it's most likely on the night stand, but you have to reach for it. If you are over sixty, it's probably in another room. I'll call my mom and she won't answer the phone. She'll call me back and say, "Sorry, I was lying down in bed and my phone was charging in the kitchen." Why isn't her phone next to her bed like a normal person's?

Regardless of how close it is, most people start their day by grabbing their phone. It begins with seeing what text messages they might have missed. Next, they take a quick look at social media to scroll through all the junk people are posting and complaining about. Third, they read all the "he said she said" comments on the latest debate. After getting out of bed, they turn on the news and hear all the horrible things happening in the world. Finally, they get in the car and listen to NPR on the way to work.

If that sounds like a familiar morning routine for you, think about what is priming your life. Is that going to help you live and walk in freedom? What if you changed your morning routine? Imagine if you woke up in the morning, picked up your Bible, read a chapter of God's Word, spent 10-15 minutes in prayer and listened to worship music on your way to work. How could those simple changes enhance your emotional health and impact your life?

FOOTNOTES

1. https://www.vox.com/first-person/2017/8/8/16112864/recidivism-rate-jail-prostitution-break-cycle

2. https://www.webmd.com/a-to-z-guides/hematidrosis-hematohidrosis#1

3. For more on the priming effect read Before you know it: The unconscious reasons we do what we do by John Bargh PH

FEEL FREE 16

LIVE FREE

Let's return to the example of Jesus in the Garden of Gethsemane we were examining in the last chapter. When Jesus was under extreme emotional stress and pressure, the first thing He did was pray. The second thing Jesus did was surround himself with the right people. Jesus didn't take all the disciples with him to the garden. He took Peter, James, and John. When we are in a stressful situation, we need to be selective on who we hang out with.

When the pressure is on, we can't be around negative people. These people are full of doubt and unbelief and only want to take without adding anything of value to our lives. We have to be selective with who surrounds us. When we are under emotional stress, there are some people who need to be sent to voicemail. It is okay, really! If you feel worse after talking to them, hit the red button when they call. If they don't speak faith, hope, and encouragement...red button!

There are some people who just aren't Monday morning people. When certain names pop up on caller ID on a Monday, it's like, "Nope. I'll call you Friday afternoon when I'm happier because I can't handle you on Monday morning." Emotions are more contagious than the flu so surround yourself with the right people.

DON'T HANG OUT WITH ANGRY PEOPLE; DON'T KEEP COMPANY WITH HOTHEADS. BAD TEMPER IS CONTAGIOUS— DON'T GET INFECTED.
PROVERBS 22:24 MESSAGE

Dr. Don Colbert did a study where three people sat in a circle silently for two minutes. Within two minutes, the most emotionally charged person transmitted his mood to the other people without saying a word. Whatever mood the emotionally charged person was experiencing was felt and experienced by the other people.[1] Emotions are contagious. Surrounding yourself with people who always have their Jack coming out of the box will cause Jack to come out of your box more often. It's a lot easier for people to pull you down than it is for

EMOTIONS ARE MORE CONTAGIOUS THAN THE FLU SO SURROUND YOURSELF WITH THE RIGHT PEOPLE.

you to pull them up. That's why Corinthians says:

DO NOT BE DECEIVED. BAD COMPANY CORRUPTS GOOD MORALS.
1 CORINTHIANS 15:33 RGT

We become like the people we hang out with on a regular basis. If we spend time with those who gossip, judge, and commiserate, in time, we will resemble them. More than any other single factor, the people we associate with will influence the person we become. We will inevitably take on the habits, attitudes, beliefs, and worldview of the people we surround ourselves with.

The dangerous part is that it's unlikely you'll even notice. This change in our character happens gradually over time. That's why Scripture says, "Don't be deceived." Just because you can't see it happening doesn't mean it's not happening. Like weight gain, character change sneaks up on you one ounce at a time. People do not drastically pull you off course in an instant, but little by little over time. If negative influences were drastic, we would fight back. Instead they nudge us little by little until we are finally pulled off course. We need to make sure to surround ourselves with the right people.

EXPRESS YOUR EMOTIONS

The third thing we see Jesus do is honestly express His feelings. Jesus said, "If there is any other way, take this cup from me." In other words, I don't want to do this so if there is a plan B, now is the time to show me. We have to be honest with God about our feelings because we can't effectively deal with our emotions if we deny them. Managing our emotions IS NOT stuffing them in our mind closet. It is not pretending things are fine while anger is seething on the inside. People who repress their pain never heal from it. In order to deal with your emotions, you have to acknowledge them and genuinely express them to God.

The struggle is that honesty doesn't come naturally to us. In marketing, every business has a slogan. Some slogans are good, some are bad, and some aren't even close to being true. McDonalds: Because you only have $4. Yellow pages: Here, you throw this away. Netflix: Spend more time searching than actually watching. Chick-fil-A: You always crave it on Sunday. Walmart: A low-class version of Target. Target: Where you pay a little more to avoid going to Wal-mart. That level of honesty would feel bazaar for a company to advertise, but they have to know, right?

Some companies don't have honest slogans just like we aren't always honest with how we are feel. This is especially true in churches. When you ask Christians how they're doing, the answer is always "Great," or if you're real spiritual, the answer is "I'm blessed." In church we have this idea that feelings and faith don't go together. We are taught that feelings are either right or wrong. We should feel this way, and we shouldn't feel that way. Don't feel this way! Instead, feel that way. But what happens when you don't feel great? Do you just pretend to be okay even if you're not okay?

God can't change the pretend version of yourself. God can't help you when you're hiding.

When Adam and Eve sinned in the Garden of Eden, the first thing God asked Adam was, "Where are you?" God asked this because God can't fix our problems if we're hiding. He can only help when you come out from hiding and get honest. God was really saying, "Would you stop trying to sow fig leaves together to manage this on your own? Come out from hiding. I can fix this because before you created the problem, I already had the solution."

The Bible says Jesus was slain before the foundation of the world (Revelation 13:8). In other words, before Adam and Eve created the problem, God already had the solution. He has the solution for what you're dealing with too, but He can't help you if you're hiding. God can't get you where you need to be if you are acting like you're already there. God can't heal your heartache if you are acting like it's already healed. God can't deliver you if you're in denial. But if you'll feel it, God will heal it. If you allow yourself to feel it and you express it to God, He will heal it. That's why we need to be honest with God about the reality of how we feel. He is loving and gracious enough to handle the raw versions of us. Don't hold back, get real with God, and give Him the opportunity to free the real you.

PURSUE PURPOSE

The last thing we see Jesus do in the garden is choose God's purpose even when He didn't feel like it. Jesus said, "Yet not what I will, but what You will." In other words, Jesus was saying "I don't want to do this but nevertheless not my will but yours." Jesus didn't allow His emotions to dictate His decisions. He felt and experienced all the pain and anguish, but He didn't let it determine His course of action. He continued to pursue God's purpose for His life.

Have you ever seen greyhound track racing? There's a mechanical rabbit kept in front of the dogs to make sure they run in the right direction. The rabbit is just in front of the dogs so they never quite catch it. They chase it all the way around the track. Once at a track in Florida, as the dogs went into the first turn, a short in the electrical system caused the rabbit to explode.

YOUR HIGHEST LEVEL OF FULFILLMENT IS NOT WHEN YOU RECEIVE FROM OTHERS BUT WHEN YOU GIVE YOUR LIFE AWAY TO OTHERS.

All of a sudden, the dogs didn't know what to do. There was no rabbit to chase. Some of the dogs sat down on the track. A couple of them tried to run through a fence and ended up getting hurt. Other dogs barked at the people in the stands. Not a single dog finished the race.[3]

This is an accurate depiction of what happens to us when we aren't pursuing God's purpose for our lives. We become stagnant. We end up hurting ourselves and fighting with others because we have nothing to chase after. We are led by your emotions because we don't have a purpose bigger than ourselves to move us in the right direction. Without a purpose, it's easy to get pulled off track.

WHERE THERE IS NO VISION FROM GOD, THE PEOPLE RUN WILD, BUT THOSE WHO ADHERE TO GOD'S INSTRUCTION KNOW GENUINE HAPPINESS.
PROVERBS 29:18 VOICE

Other translations of Proverbs 29:18 say with no purpose, people cast off restraint or live without self control. Without God-given purpose, we end up driven by our emotions. That's why pursuing God's purpose is essential to living in freedom. A person without a vision for the future will always return to the past. We have to keep God's purpose in front of us.

God's purpose always involves serving others. It's using our gifts to make a difference in the lives of others. Helping others get free helps you live free. Nelson Mandela said, "For to be free is not merely to cast off one's chains, but to live in a way that respects and enhances the freedom of others." God wants you to enhance the freedom of others. When you do this, you actually experience the highest level of joy and fulfillment in life. God designed you so that you will not experience fulfillment until you're making a difference in the lives of others. Your highest level of fulfillment is not when you receive from others but when you give your life away to others. Your greatest joy is found making an impact in the lives of others, and it also enables you to live free.

LOOKING UNTO JESUS, THE AUTHOR AND FINISHER OF OUR FAITH, WHO FOR THE JOY THAT WAS SET BEFORE HIM ENDURED THE CROSS, DESPISING THE SHAME, AND HAS SAT DOWN AT THE RIGHT HAND OF THE THRONE OF GOD.
HEBREWS 12:2

LIVE FREE

In the Garden of Gethsemane, Jesus was overwhelmed with sorrow to the point of death. He knew the agony before Him. His response remained, "Not my will be done but yours" because of the joy that was set before Him. The joy that was set before Him was you. He knew that in choosing obedience to the cross, you could have a relationship with Him. Even under extreme pressure, Jesus didn't allow His emotions to govern His decision. He felt and experienced all the pain and anguish, but He didn't let it move Him outside of God's plan. Jesus kept Father God's purpose in front of Him. Go and discover your God given purpose. Pursue living out that purpose with all you are. In that sacred pursuit, you will be empowered to truly live free.

FOOTNOTES

1. Deadly Emotions: Understand the Mind-Body-Spirit Connection that Can Heal or Destroy You by Dr. Don Colbert

2. https://honestslogans.com/

3. It: How churches and leaders can get it and keep it. By Craig Groeschel, pg 39-40

EPILOGUE

Feeling free is not the end goal; it's just the beginning. The purpose of freedom is to serve God completely. To remove anything hindering us from giving ourselves wholly to His desire for our lives. Obtaining freedom without walking in purpose is equivalent to Israel coming out of Egypt but not entering the Promised Land. The purpose of being freed from slavery in Egypt was to serve God in the Promised Land.

AND THE LORD SPOKE TO MOSES, "GO TO PHARAOH AND SAY TO HIM, 'THUS SAYS THE LORD: "LET MY PEOPLE GO, THAT THEY MAY SERVE ME."

EXODUS 8:1

EPILOGUE

AND THE LORD SAID TO MOSES, "RISE EARLY IN THE MORNING AND STAND BEFORE PHARAOH AS HE COMES OUT TO THE WATER. THEN SAY TO HIM, 'THUS SAYS THE LORD: "LET MY PEOPLE GO, THAT THEY MAY SERVE ME."

EXODUS 8:20

THEN THE LORD SAID TO MOSES, "RISE EARLY IN THE MORNING AND STAND BEFORE PHARAOH, AND SAY TO HIM, 'THUS SAYS THE LORD GOD OF THE HEBREWS: "LET MY PEOPLE GO, THAT THEY MAY SERVE ME."

EXODUS 9:13

SO MOSES AND AARON CAME IN TO PHARAOH AND SAID TO HIM, "THUS SAYS THE LORD GOD OF THE HEBREWS: 'HOW LONG WILL YOU REFUSE TO HUMBLE YOURSELF BEFORE ME? LET MY PEOPLE GO, THAT THEY MAY SERVE ME."

EXODUS 10:3

God's purpose is made pretty clear from this sampling of scripture. Setting Israel free wasn't just so they could be free; it was so they could be free to serve Him. God knew that Israel couldn't fully serve Him as long as they were slaves in Egypt. God wants us to feel free because He knows we can't fully serve Him and fulfill His purpose for our lives while we are in bondage.

We want to be free so we don't have to live in guilt, shame, and condemnation. We want to be free so we aren't weighed down by worry, fear, and anxiety. We want to be loosed from negative emotions so we feel better. God also wants us to be unfettered so we can freely give ourselves to His purpose.

In fact, if you get free but don't give yourself to God's purpose, it's only a matter of time before you find yourself back in bondage. If we make life about ourselves after experiencing freedom, weare still in prison, we've just switched rooms. Living a selfish life after being set free is still bondage. Freedom is not doing whatever we want, it's doing what God wants. It's being available for God's purpose to be fulfilled.

THE PURPOSE OF FEELING FREE IS TO CARRY JESUS INTO YOUR SPHERE OF INFLUENCE.

There is a great analogy of the purpose of freedom found in Matthew chapter 21. In this chapter Jesus is getting ready to make His triumphal entry into Jerusalem.

> NOW WHEN THEY DREW NEAR JERUSALEM, AND CAME TO BETHPHAGE, AT THE MOUNT OF OLIVES, THEN JESUS SENT TWO DISCIPLES, SAYING TO THEM, "GO INTO THE VILLAGE OPPOSITE YOU, AND IMMEDIATELY YOU WILL FIND A DONKEY TIED, AND A COLT WITH HER. LOOSE THEM AND BRING THEM TO ME.
> MATTHEW 21:1-2

Jesus sent the disciples to find and loose the donkey so that He could ride the donkey into Jerusalem. Before the donkey could be used by Jesus, it first had to be loosed. Only when you are loosed from your chains can you walk in your calling. The enemy tries to bind people with chains of addiction, low self-esteem, fear, guilt, and shame to hold them from what they were created for. You must be loosed so that you can carry out your destiny.

EPILOGUE

Notice the disciples weren't instructed to loose the donkey and set it free so that it could go wherever it wanted. It was freed for a purpose: to carry Jesus into Jerusalem.

WHEN JESUS ENTERED THE CITY ON THE DONKEY THE WHOLE CITY WAS MOVED.
MATTHEW 21:10

The purpose of feeling free is to carry Jesus into your sphere of influence. God wants to move in the education system, government, media, arts, entertainment, and business, but He needs someone to carry Him.

God wants you to be a missionary to your sphere of influence. When people hear the word missionary, they tend to think about quitting their job and moving to another country. Missionary is more of a mindset than a location. It's being intentional about bringing the kingdom of God into your place of influence. As Jesus sat on the donkey, it became transportation for Him into the city. He wants your life to be the vehicle that carries Him into your circle.

The end goal of freedom is to see Jesus move in the lives of your family, friends, workplace, and church. It's to be used by God to draw people to Jesus. God wants you to feel free so that you carry His grace and goodness into the lives of others.